Harcourt Language

Practice Book

Grade 2

Orlando Boston Dallas Chicago San Diego

Visit *The Learning Site!*
www.harcourtschool.com

Printed in the United States of America

ISBN 0-15-317984-8 3 4 5 6 7 8 9 10 082 2003 2002 2001

Contents

Name ______________________________

What Is a Sentence?

A. Draw a line under each sentence.

1. The family is building a treehouse.

2. Mandy hammers the nails.
3. paints the wood.
4. Dad sews drapes.
5. The little sister

B. Use the words from the box to make complete sentences.

They	**The girl**	**looks better**
are cleaning the room		**puts toys away**

6. The children are cleaning the room.
7. The boy puts toys Away.
8. The giRl sweeps the floor.
9. The room looks better.
10. They clean well.

TRY THIS! Write two sentences that tell what you do to clean up your room.

Name ____________________

Word Order in a Sentence

A. Read the groups of words. Underline the sentences that are in the correct order.

1. Gloria likes oranges.
2. apple juice always drinks Jem.
3. favorite her drink It is.
4. Bananas are tasty.
5. Luis likes grapes best.

B. Write each group of words in an order that makes sense.

6. food. Bob likes spicy

Bob likes spicyfood.

7. lots of Sue eats fruit.

Sue eats lots of fruit.

8. Jake to drink wants milk.

Jake wants to drink milk

TRY THIS! Think about a healthful food that you like to eat. Write sentences to tell about the food.

Name ____________________

Beginning and Ending a Sentence

A. Read each pair of sentences. Circle the sentence that begins and ends correctly.

1. The girl picks red and yellow flowers.
   the girl picks red and yellow flowers.

2. she wants to give them to her mom
   She wants to give them to her mom.

3. The flowers smell sweet.
   The flowers smell sweet

B. Write each sentence correctly.

4. the baby can clap

   The baby can Clap.

5. the boy knows how to walk

   The boy Knows how to walk.

6. my big sister writes her name

   My big Sister writes her name.

TRY THIS! Draw pictures of three people you know. Write a sentence about each person.

Name ___________________________

Extra Practice

A. Underline each group of words that is a sentence.

1. I am the oldest child.
   am the oldest child.

2. The tallest in the family
   Jack is the tallest in the family.

B. Write the words in an order that makes sense.

3. fix Mom can anything.

   Mom can fix anything

4. cooks Dad dinner night. each

   Dad cooks dinner each night.

C. Write each sentence correctly.

5. the boys want to build a ship

   The boys want to build a ship.

6. they ask Grandma to help them

   They ask Grandma to help them.

Name ______________________________

Using the Parts of Your Book

Contents

Use the table of contents to answer each question.

1. How many chapters does the book have? 4

2. What is the name of the first chapter?

Here Comes Buster.

3. On what page does Chapter 2 begin? 9

4. What is the name of Chapter 3?

Off to School

5. What chapter is called "Buster Saves the Day"? 4

TRY THIS! Think about a book you might like to write. Make up a title page and table of contents for it.

Name ______________________________

What Are the Parts of a Sentence?

A. Write a naming part to complete each sentence.

1. Sue go to school every day.

2. Jo is my friend.

3. Sue and Jo have fun on the playground.

4. They line up for lunch.

5. She has a tasty lunch.

B. Write a telling part to complete each sentence.

6. My teacher is nice.

7. My friend runs fast.

8. The school is fun.

9. My class is Small.

10. The playground is fun.

TRY THIS! Think about three classmates. Write a sentence about each one. Make sure each sentence has a naming part and a telling part.

Name ______________________________

Naming Parts and Telling Parts

A. Read each sentence. Circle the naming part of each sentence. Underline the telling part.

1. School is open five days a week.
2. My teacher checks who is here.
3. I read books.
4. My class learns new things each day.
5. We eat lunch at noon.

B. Use a naming part or telling part from the box to complete each sentence.

The children	**help after school**	
Robert	**has a good class**	**Jane**

6. Ms. Smith has a good class.
7. Robert always comes to school on time.
8. Jane does her homework neatly.
9. The boys help after school.
10. The children walk in a straight line.

TRY THIS! Write a note to a friend. Tell about something you did. Be sure to write at least two sentences.

Name ______________________________

Combining Parts of Sentences

Use *and* to join each pair of sentences. Write the new sentence.

1. Pumpkins are ripe. Apples are ripe.

Pumpkins and apples are ripe.

2. Farms sell pumpkins. Stores sell pumpkins.

Farms and Stores sell pumpkins.

3. My friends pick apples. I pick apples.

My friends and I pick apples.

4. Dad can make a pie. Mom can make a pie.

Dad and Mom can make a pie.

5. Apples taste sweet. Pumpkins taste sweet.

Apples and pumpkins taste sweet.

6. The boys eat pie. The girls eat pie.

The boys and girls eat pie.

TRY THIS! Think about two friends. What can they both do? What do they both have? Write one sentence telling about both friends. Use *and* to combine the naming parts.

Name ______________________________

Extra Practice

A. Circle the naming part in each sentence.

1. Board games are fun.

2. You have to play with friends.

3. Each game is different.

4. I win sometimes.

B. Circle the telling part in each sentence.

5. My friends win other times.

6. I like other games, too.

7. Tag is fun.

8. My friends can not catch me!

C. Use *and* to join each pair of sentences. Write the new sentence.

9. Joe can play checkers. Tina can play checkers.

Joe and Tina cAn play checkers.

10. My sisters play ball. I play ball.

My sisters and I play ball.

Name ______________________________

Using ABC Order

Use the thesaurus page to answer each question.

afraid filled with fear
frightened *scared*
cry to shed tears
sob *weep*
eat to take food into the body
gobble *taste*
pretty nice-looking or beautiful
beautiful *lovely*
take to move or carry something
bring *carry*
walk to move by using the feet
step *stroll*

1. Which word comes before *take*?

pretty

2. What is the first word on this list?

afraid

3. Where would the word *sad* go?

after pretty before take

4. Would the word *clear* come before or after *cry*?

before

5. Name a word that would come after *eat* but before *pretty*.

fear

6. What word comes after *cry*? eat

TRY THIS! Make your own thesaurus. List ten words and their synonyms. Put them in alphabetical order.

Name ______________________________

Different Kinds of Sentences

A. Read each sentence. Write whether it is a statement or a question.

1. The class is putting on a play. statement
2. Does Theo have the lead? question
3. Is Mr. Garcia the director? question
4. Donna has a big part. statement
5. Will she remember her lines? question

B. Write each sentence from the box under the correct heading.

Statement	Question
The play is about a prince.	Does the prince find her?

Does the prince find her?
The play is about a prince.

TRY THIS! Think about a play or television show you have seen. Write two questions about it. Then write a statement to answer each question.

Name ____________________

Using Statements and Questions

A. Write an *S* beside each statement. Write a *Q* beside each question.

1. Who is playing the piano? 

2. Kareem is playing the piano. 

3. What is the name of the song? 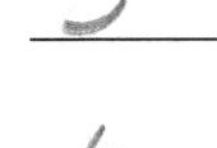

4. I wish I could play like that. 

5. Have you ever taken lessons? 

B. Write each sentence correctly.

6. Max drew this flower

Max drew this flower.

7. is it a rose

Is it a rose?

8. how did he draw it

How did he draw it?

TRY THIS! Write two questions to ask a partner. Then trade papers. Write answers to your partner's questions.

Name ______________________________

Sentences That Go Together

A. Read each paragraph. Cross out the sentence that doesn't belong.

1. We learned about paintbrushes in art class. People use one kind of brush for oil paint. I read about plants in my science book. They use another kind for watercolor paint.

2. Nia is a good artist. She draws neat pictures. Nia lives on Lake Street. Then she colors the pictures with crayons. Sometimes she even paints them.

B. Write the sentence from the box that belongs in the paragraph.

3. Maria is in the school play. She wants to play her part well. She practices her lines often.

Her brother helps her remember the lines.

The costume is yellow.
Jeff plays the piano.
She practices her lines often.

TRY THIS! Write a paragraph about something you do well. Then read the sentences to make sure they all go together.

Name ______________________________

Extra Practice

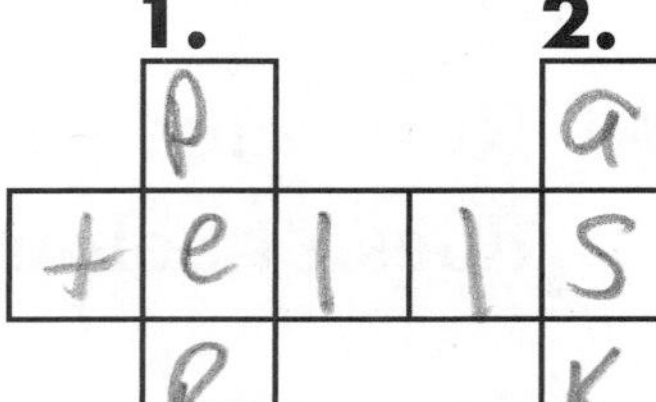
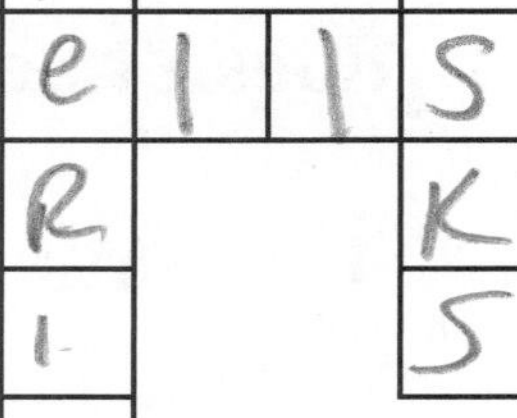

A. Write the correct word to fill in each blank. Then write the word in the puzzle.

1. A statement ends with a period.
2. A question is a sentence that asks something.
3. A statement is a sentence that tells something.

B. Write each sentence correctly.

4. sami likes to play tennis

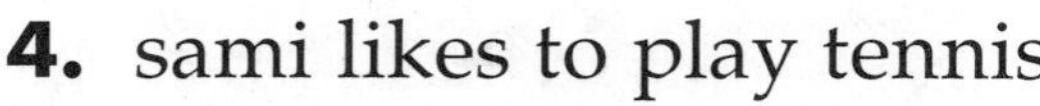

Sami likes to play tennis.

5. she plays each Saturday

6. is she going to play today

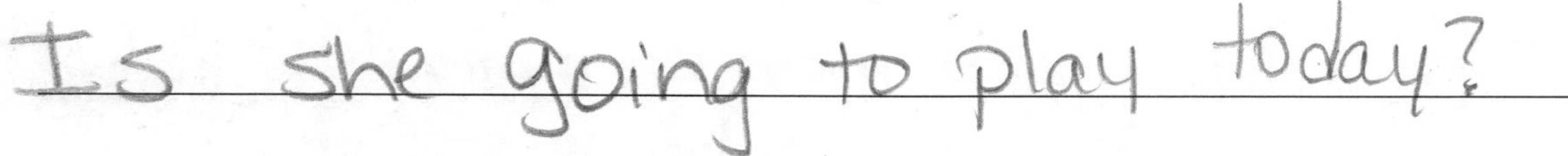

C. Underline the sentence that belongs with the group of sentences from Part B.

7. Sami's game is not far from here.

Sami used to play soccer.

Name ___________________________

Homophones

A. Draw a line to match each word in Column A with its homophone in Column B.

Column A	Column B
1. too	be
2. hare	know
3. no	two
4. bee	hair
5. knows	nose

B. Circle the word in ( ) that fits best in each sentence.

6. I **(need, knead)** the book.

7. **(Hear, Here)** it is.

8. My mom **(red, read)** it.

9. **(Eye, I)** did, too.

10. The book is **(for, four)** my dad.

TRY THIS! Write three silly sentences using these pairs of words: *tail* and *tale*, *whole* and *hole*, and *shoe* and *shoo*.

Name ______________________

More Kinds of Sentences

A. Read the sentences. Write the exclamations.

1. Do you hear the drum?

   I hear the drum!

2. Bill plays so loudly!

   ____

3. The band is great!

   ____

B. Read each pair of sentences. Write the command.

4. My father is in a band.
   Hand the CD to me.

   Hand the CD to me.

5. Listen to this.
   Is that your father playing?

   Listen to this.

TRY THIS! Think about the type of music you like best. Write an exclamation that shows how you feel about the music.

Name ______________________

Exclamations and Commands

A. Write whether each sentence is an exclamation or a command.

1. Hurry to the table. command
2. What a yummy meal! exclamation
3. Look at the pizza. command
4. This is great! exclamation

B. Write the exclamations and the commands. Use the correct end marks.

5. Pass the carrots to me

Pass the carrots to me.

6. The cheese is hot

The cheese is hot!

7. Pizza is my favorite

Pizza is my favorite!

TRY THIS! Draw a picture of something that could happen at school. Write a command and an exclamation about your picture.

Name ______________________________

Using Different Kinds of Sentences

A. Draw a line from each sentence in Column A to the word in Column B that tells what kind of sentence it is.

Column A	Column B
1. Feed the dog.	question
2. Is it Kara's pet?	statement
3. What a beautiful animal!	command
4. Kara loves Fido.	exclamation

B. Finish each sentence. Use the word in ( ) to tell you what type of sentence to write. Use the correct end marks.

5. **(statement)** Pat and her dog have fun.

6. **(question)** When do I go home?

7. **(exclamation)** What a pretty dog!

8. **(exclamation)** It's such a pretty day!

9. **(command)** Start the game.

TRY THIS! Make a poster that tells about the students in your class. Include statements, questions, exclamations, and commands on your poster.

Name ______________________________

Extra Practice

A. Circle the commands. Underline the exclamations.

1. Look at the dancers.

2. They jump so high!

3. The dance is beautiful!

B. Write each exclamation and command correctly.

4. lily dances well

Lily dances well.

5. watch her turn

Watch her turn!

C. Change each statement into a new kind of sentence shown in ( ). Write the new sentence.

6. Lily loves to dance. **(question)**

Does Lily love to dance?

7. She does a graceful turn. **(exclamation)**

She does a graceful turn!

Name ___________________________________

Using a Computer

A. Use the words in the box to label the parts of the computer.

keyboard	monitor	printer	mouse	hard drive

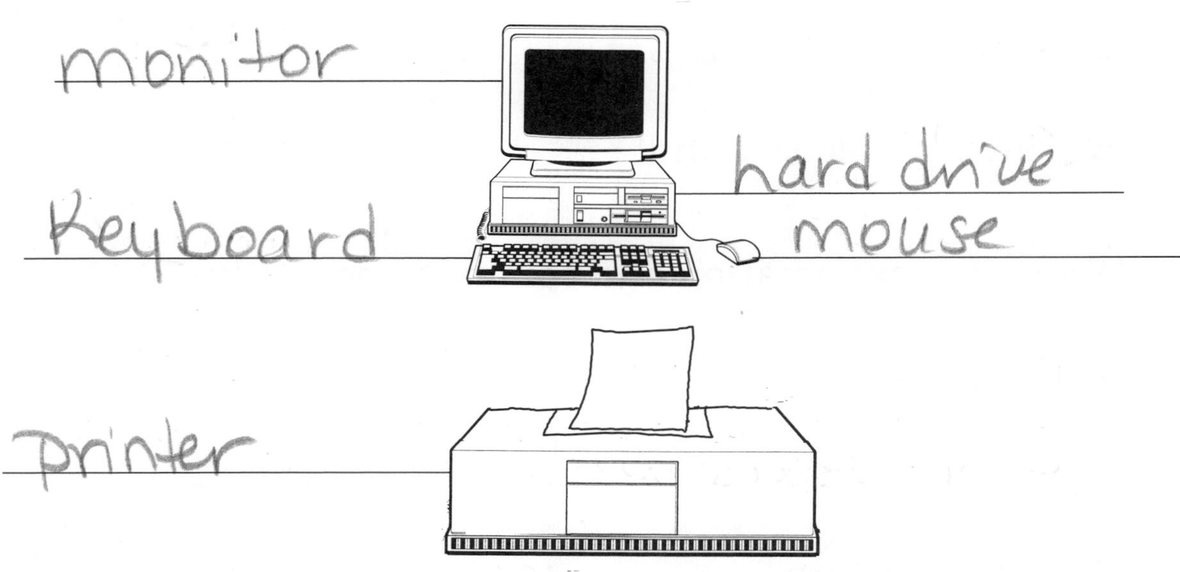

B. Type each sentence on your computer. Follow the proofreading marks to make changes to the text.

1. I have two ^cute cats.
2. ~~There~~ Their names are Haley and Leo.
3. Haley has ^soft white fur.
4. l̳eo looks like a tiger.

TRY THIS! Use the computer to write a sentence about yourself. Then go back and correct the sentence by using the cursor, keyboard, and Delete key.

Name ______________________

What Is a Noun?

A. Circle the noun in each group. Write it on the line.

1. ask book on ask
2. school over tell tell
3. with sad girl with
4. happy desk under under
5. teacher glad say Say

B. Write a noun from the box to complete each sentence.

brother	bucket	beach	castle	sand

6. The beach is fun.
7. We play in the sand.
8. I use a bucket.
9. My brother shapes the sand.
10. Our castle is nice.

TRY THIS! Write three sentences to tell about the people, places, and things you see on your way to school.

Name ______________________

Nouns for People, Places, Animals, and Things

A. Underline the noun in each sentence. Write it on the line.

1. The boy wanted to paint. boy
2. He took some paper. paper
3. He used gray paint. paint
4. He painted a whale. whale
5. It was swimming in the ocean. ocean

B. Write the noun from the box that best fits in each sentence.

picture	parents	students	paper	sea

6. Mrs. Jackson's students went to the art room.
7. They put a sheet of paper on the wall.
8. They painted a large picture.
9. It showed fish swimming in the sea.
10. The children showed it to their parents.

TRY THIS! Look around the room. Write three sentences about things you see. You may draw a picture of each thing.

Name ____________________

Using Possessive Nouns

A. Add *'s* to each word in ( ) to show ownership. Write the new word on the line.

1. We went to my **(grandmother)** grandmother's house.
2. We sat in my **(grandfather)** grandfather's chair.
3. It was my **(aunt)** aunt's birthday.
4. I took my **(uncle)** uncle's hat.
5. It looked silly on the **(baby)** baby's head.

B. Use *'s* to rewrite the underlined words in each sentence.

6. My family put the food in the truck of my dad. my dad's truck
7. I borrowed the book of José. José's book
8. I put it in the bag of my mother. my mother's bag
9. The dog of the neighbor came, too. neighbor's dog
10. Jeff put the snack of the dog in his pocket. dog's snack

TRY THIS! Write a list of things to take on a picnic. Make sure to use possessive nouns. Draw a picture of each thing.

Name ______________________

Extra Practice

A. Find the noun in each sentence. Write it on the line.

1. She likes her colorful bird. biRd

2. He never even says a word. WoRd

3. I have a small stuffed bear. bear

4. He has a lot of brown hair. haiR

B. Write a noun from the box to finish each sentence.

cat	**dog**	**hat**	**log**

5. Mark has a puppy dog.

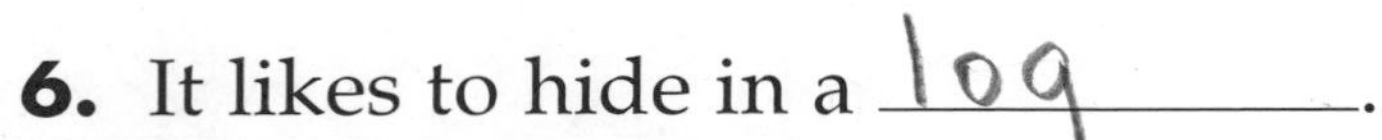

6. It likes to hide in a log.

7. Cathy has a furry Cat.

8. It likes to play with her brother's hat.

C. Add 's to make each noun in ( ) possessive. Write the sentence.

9. Have you seen my **(brother)** snake?

brother's

10. He tried to eat **(Charlie)** cake.

Charlie's

Name ______________________

Compound Nouns

A. Underline the compound noun in each sentence. Write the two nouns that make it up.

1. My uncle lives on a houseboat. house boat
2. He has a small bedroom. bed room
3. There is a short footstool. foot stool
4. There is a warm bedspread. bed spread
5. His books are in the bookcase. book case

B. Match a word in Column A with one in Column B to make a compound noun. Write the compound nouns.

	Column A	Column B
6. fireplace	fire	bone
7. back bone	back	plane
8. air plane	air	nail
9. drum stick	drum	place
10. fingernail	finger	stick

TRY THIS! Look around the classroom to find objects that are compound nouns. Write sentences using the words. Draw pictures to go with the sentences.

Name ______________________________

Nouns That Name More Than One

A. Read each sentence. Underline the noun that names more than one.

1. My grandparents let me help them.
2. We plant flowers.
3. We put seeds in the ground.
4. Roses are my favorite.
5. My grandfather plants tulips.

B. Circle the noun in ( ) that names more than one.

6. Grandfather waters the other **(plants, plant)**.
7. They grow **(pea, peas)** in the backyard.
8. **(Carrots, Carrot)** grow by the fence.
9. They have one of the best **(garden, gardens)** around.
10. They worked on it for many **(years, year)**.

TRY THIS! Think about fruits and vegetables you have eaten. Write sentences to describe the ones you like and the ones you don't like. Be sure to include words that name more than one.

Name ____________________

Making Nouns Plural

A. Write the word that names more than one.

1. one plum two plums

2. one grape five grapes

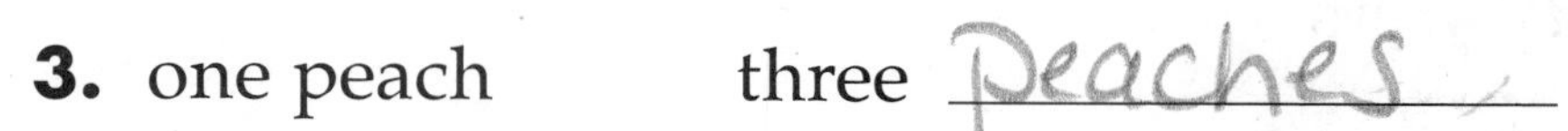

3. one peach three peaches

4. one apple four apples

5. one melon two melons

B. Add *s* or *es* to make the word in ( ) mean more than one. Write the word on the line.

6. Nancy saw a pile of **(dish)** dishes in the store.

7. They had pretty **(flower)** flowers painted on them.

8. Then she saw some **(glass)** gasses.

9. They had cute **(animal)** animals painted on them.

10. The salesman packed them in **(box)** boxes.

TRY THIS! Make a list of things you see more than one of in the classroom. Then illustrate the list.

Name ______________________________

Plural Nouns That Change Spelling

A. Draw a line from each noun that names one to the form of that noun that names more than one.

1. mouse	teeth
2. woman	men
3. tooth	women
4. child	mice
5. man	children

B. Change the spelling to make each noun in ( ) mean more than one. Write the new sentence.

6. The **(child)** went to the pet store.

The Children went to the pet store

7. The **(man)** in the store were nice.

The men in the store were nice

8. They had white **(mouse)**.

They had white mice.

TRY THIS! Write a note to a friend about an animal. Talk about parts of the animal's body. Use as many plural nouns that change spelling as you can.

Name ______________________________

Extra Practice

A. Add *s* or *es* to make the word in ( ) mean more than one.

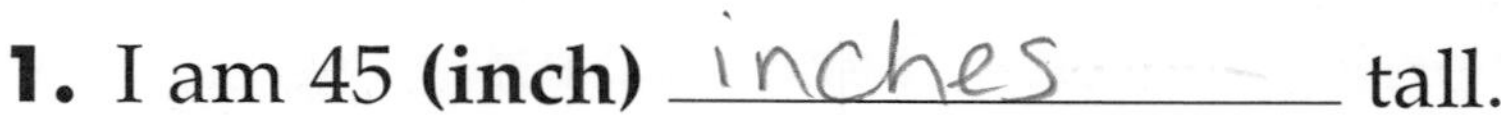

1. I am 45 **(inch)** inches tall.

2. I have two older **(sister)** sisters.

3. A pair of **(glass)** glasses helps me see.

4. I have two **(dog)** dogs.

B. Change the spelling to make each underlined word mean more than one. Write the new sentence.

5. Tara drew two <u>woman</u>.

Tara drew two women

6. Anton traced his <u>foot</u>.

Anton traced his feet

7. They both drew <u>wolf</u>.

they both drew wolves

8. The <u>child</u> like to draw.

The children like to draw.

Name ____________________

Finding Words in a Dictionary

A. Look at each set of guide words. Write a word from the box that could be on that dictionary page.

free cent bone leaf hen

1. big burn bone
2. card cook cent
3. late line leaf
4. happy hurry hen
5. face fun free

B. Circle the word in each group that could be on a dictionary page with the guide words *lad* and *land*.

6. map, lamp, lend
7. lame, limp, boy
8. lost, left, ladder
9. learn, lady, lose
10. lake, light, luck

TRY THIS! Look at a dictionary. Write the guide words for three pages. Use some of the words to write two sentences.

Name ____________________

What Is a Proper Noun?

A. Underline the proper noun in each sentence.

1. My name is Angela.
2. I live in New York City.
3. My friend Sara is on a trip.
4. She will be in Texas for a week.
5. I'm taking care of her cat Sage.

B. Write a proper noun to finish each sentence.

6. My favorite cousin is Jill.
7. He lives in the state of Alabama.
8. The name of his town is Saks.
9. My teacher is Ed.
10. If I had a pet bird, I would name it Jimmy.

TRY THIS! Plan a story. Write sentences to tell about the two main characters. What are their names? Where do they live? Use proper nouns.

Name ______________________________

People, Places, and Animals

A. Write the proper noun in ( ) correctly.

1. My friend, **(dan thorpe)**, needed help. Dan Thorpe

2. His dog, **(buster)**, ran off after a squirrel. Buster

3. My brother, **(ed)**, came with us. Ed

4. We ran to **(oak park)**. Oak Park

5. We found the dog at **(spring pond)**! Spring Park

B. Write a proper noun to complete each sentence.

6. My name is Keri.

7. I live in the town of Danielsville.

8. That's in the state of Alabama.

TRY THIS! Write sentences about a time you helped a friend or a family member. Use proper nouns.

Name ______________________________

Days, Months, and Holidays

A. Underline the names of days, months, and holidays in the sentences.

1. Today is the last day of June.
2. Jimmy can't wait for the Fourth of July.
3. Our picnic is on Sunday at Oak Park.
4. Our last picnic was on Memorial Day.
5. We are baking cookies on Saturday.

B. Write each day, month, or holiday correctly.

6. This is the last week of november. November
7. My mom's favorite holiday is on thursday. Thursday
8. Do you like thanksgiving, too? Thanksgiving
9. My favorite holiday is in december. December
10. We will start decorating next friday. Friday

TRY THIS! Write sentences about your favorite month. Why is it your favorite? What special days do you enjoy during that month? How do you help make them special?

Name ______________________

Extra Practice

A. Use proper nouns from the box to complete the sentences.

The girl	Rover	the dog
Pet Palace	the store	Jennifer

1. Jennifer has a huge dog.
2. She walks Rover twice a day.
3. Today she went to Pet Palace for a new leash.

B. Underline each letter that should be a capital letter. Then write the proper nouns correctly.

4. Her brother ben drove her. Ben
5. They drove down pine road. Pine Road

C. Circle each day, month, and holiday that is not correct. Write it correctly on the line.

6. Jen goes to camp in july. July
7. She will be back before labor day. Labor Day
8. I'll walk Fritz each monday. Monday

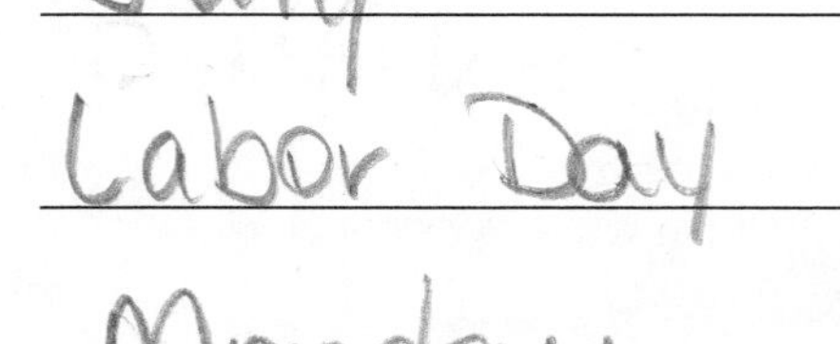

Name ______________________

Abbreviations and Titles

A. Write the abbreviation for each day or month.

1. September Sept.

2. Thursday Thurs.

3. Tuesday Tues.

4. December Dec.

5. August Aug.

6. Sunday Sun.

B. Underline each title that should have a capital letter and end with a period. Write each title and name correctly.

7. mr and mrs Lee took Bootsy to the vet.

Mr. and Mrs. Lee

8. Bootsy's vet is dr Anderson.

Dr. Anderson

TRY THIS! Plan your week. List the abbreviations for the days of the week. Next to each abbreviation, write what you would like to do that day.

Name ________________________________

What Is a Pronoun?

A. Underline the pronoun in each sentence.

1. They pick up trash in the park.
2. She holds the bag for Carlos.
3. He places the trash in the bag.
4. When it gets heavy, Sara uses a new bag.
5. They are working hard.

B. Write a pronoun from the box to complete each sentence.

They	**He**	**It**	**She**

6. She likes helping Carlos.
7. He asked her to be his partner.
8. They offered to clean the park.
9. It is a project for their school.
10. He hopes the park will stay clean.

TRY THIS! Write two sentences about ways you and your classmates could help at school. Use pronouns in your sentences.

Name ______________________________

He, She, It, and *They*

A. Draw a line from the word or words in column A to the correct pronoun in column B.

Column A	Column B
1. Pedro and Miguel	it
2. Mark	they
3. the table	she
4. my mother	he

B. Write a pronoun for the word or words in ( ).

5. **(My grandmother)** had a birthday party. She

6. **(My aunts and uncles)** surprised her with a cake. They

7. Then **(my father)** sang a song for her. He

8. **(My cousins)** played the music. they

9. **(My grandmother)** danced with me. She

10. **(The party)** was wonderful! It

TRY THIS! Write two sentences about your classmates. Then change all the nouns to pronouns, and write the sentences again.

Name ________________________________

I and *Me*

A. Write *I* or *me* to complete each sentence.

1. My mom had a surprise for <u>Me</u>.

2. My mom and <u>I</u> went to the circus.

3. <u>I</u> brought Mikio, too.

4. Mikio and <u>I</u> saw the tumbling clowns.

5. The circus made <u>me</u> very happy.

B. Choose *I* or *me* to complete each sentence. Write the new sentence.

6. Mikio and **(I, me)** went to the zoo.

Mikio and I went to the zoo

7. **(I, Me)** liked the penguins.

I liked the penguins

8. They made **(I, me)** laugh.

They made me laugh.

TRY THIS! Write three sentences about a school trip you took. Be sure to use pronouns. Draw a picture if you want.

Name ______________________________

Extra Practice

A. Write a pronoun to replace the underlined word or words in each sentence. Then write the pronoun in the puzzle.

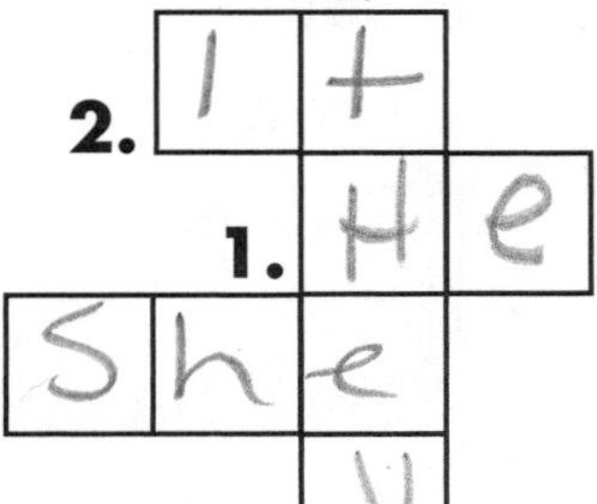

1. My dad brought in my birthday gift.
   He

2. The gift was in a big box. It

3. My mom placed it in the living room. She

4. Mom and Dad told me it was a surprise. they

B. Change the underlined word or words in each sentence to a pronoun. Rewrite the sentence.

5. My friends all came.
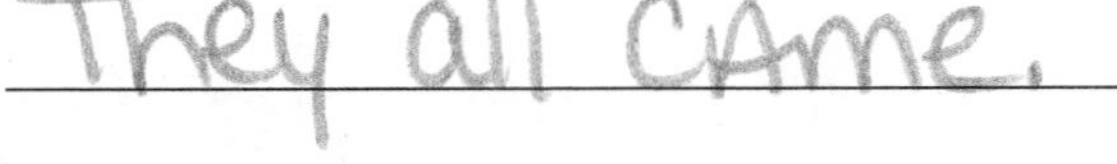

6. Bob came, too.

7. A new bike was in the box!

C. Write the correct word to complete each sentence.

8. My sister gave **(I, me)** Me a present.

9. **(I, Me)** I gave her a hug.

10. My sister and **(I, me)** I are good friends.

Name ______________________________

Sending E-mail

Answer the questions about the e-mail message.

To: stephanie@email.com
From: beth@email.com
Subject: My new puppy

Dear Stephanie,

I am so excited! I just got a new puppy. Her name is Bailey. Right now she is very small, but she will get a little bigger before long. She has white fur with colored spots on it.

I hope you can come and meet her soon!

Love,
Beth

1. Who is the writer of this message? Beth
2. What is Beth's address? beth@email.com
3. What is the subject? My new puppy
4. Who is getting this message? Stephanie
5. What is Beth's e-mail about? Beth's puppy

TRY THIS! Write an e-mail message that you would like to send to someone. Then ask your teacher or parent if you can send it. Type your message on the computer, and send it to a friend.

Name ____________________

What Is a Verb?

A. Underline the verb in each sentence.

1. The park rangers hike to the lake.
2. One ranger points to some raccoons.
3. One raccoon takes some food.
4. It washes the food in the water.
5. The raccoons eat the food.

B. Write the verb from the box that best completes each sentence.

pet	find	sleeps	name	drinks

6. The firefighters find a tiny, lost kitten.
7. The kitten drinks a whole bowl of milk.
8. The firefighters pet the kitten's fur.
9. They name the kitten Sparky.
10. Sparky sleeps in a firefighter's hat!

TRY THIS! Write four sentences about the things a kitten may do. Underline the verbs.

Name ______________________________

Adding *s* or *es* to Verbs

Write the verb from the box that best completes each sentence. Add *s* or *es* if you need to do so.

sleep	**roll**	**eat**	**brush**	**feed**
close	**drive**	**kiss**	**watch**	**toss**

1. She drives the tractor to the field.

2. Nancy feeds the kitten.

3. Martin watches the ducks in the pond.

4. The pig rolls in the mud.

5. Jim tosses hay to the cows.

6. The man brushes the horse.

7. The cows eat hay.

8. The dog sleeps near the cow.

9. Mary feeds the hens.

10. She closes the barn door.

TRY THIS! Write three sentences about things that happen on a farm. Use some verbs from the box above.

Name ___

Combining Sentences with Verbs

A. Draw a line from the sentence in column A to the sentence in column B that has the same naming part.

Column A	Column B
1. The birds land.	**a.** Hiro watches the birds.
2. Hiro looks out the window.	**b.** The birds eat birdseed.
3. A cat sees the birds.	**c.** A cat chases them away.

B. Use *and* to join each sentence pair above that has the same naming part. Write the new sentences on the lines.

4. The birds land And eat birdseed
5. Hiro looks out the window and watches the birds
6. A cat sees the birds And chases them away.

TRY THIS! Write two sentences about an animal. Make sure the sentences have the same naming part. Then trade papers with a classmate. Join the sentences by using *and*.

Name ______________________________

Extra Practice

A. Underline the verb in each sentence. Then write it in the puzzle.

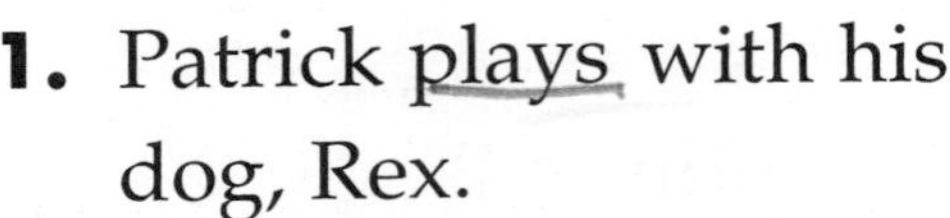

1. Patrick plays with his dog, Rex.

2. They tease each other.

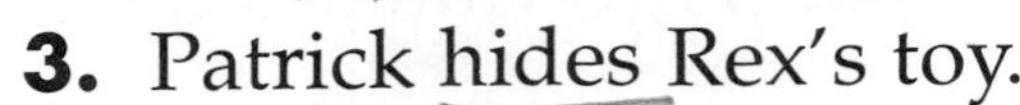

3. Patrick hides Rex's toy.

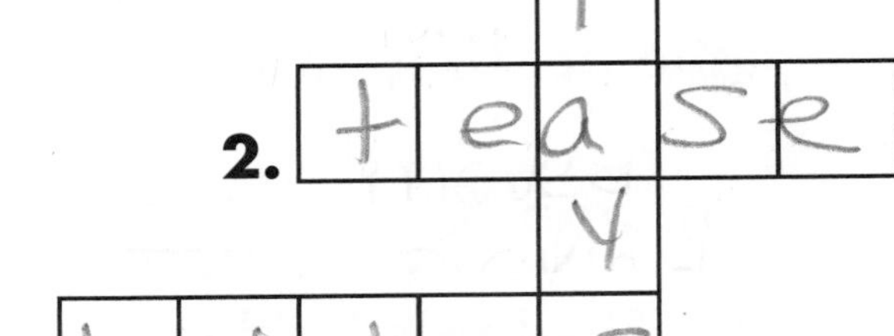

B. Write the verb from the box that best completes each sentence. Add *s* or *es* if you need to do so.

put	get	rush

4. The dog gets the toy from its hiding place.

5. The dog puts the toy near Patrick.

C. Use *and* to join the sentences. Write the new sentence.

6. The dog watches Patrick. The dog grabs the toy.

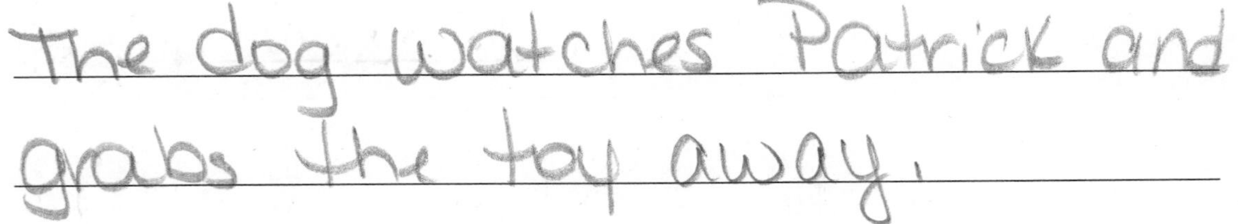

7. Dad smiles. Dad gives Patrick another toy.

Name ____________________

Synonyms for Verbs

A. Write the verbs from the box to complete the chart.

yell	nap	~~travel~~	~~run~~	snooze	whisper

synonyms for *sleep*	synonyms for *go*	synonyms for *say*
1. nap	**3.** travel	**5.** yell
2. Snooze	**4.** run	**6.** wisper

B. Choose the best synonym from the chart for each underlined word. Write the synonym in the puzzle. Add *s* if you need to do so.

7. Mom says, "Good night."
8. The baby sleeps each afternoon.
9. We say, "Hooray! We won!"
10. A family goes in a race.

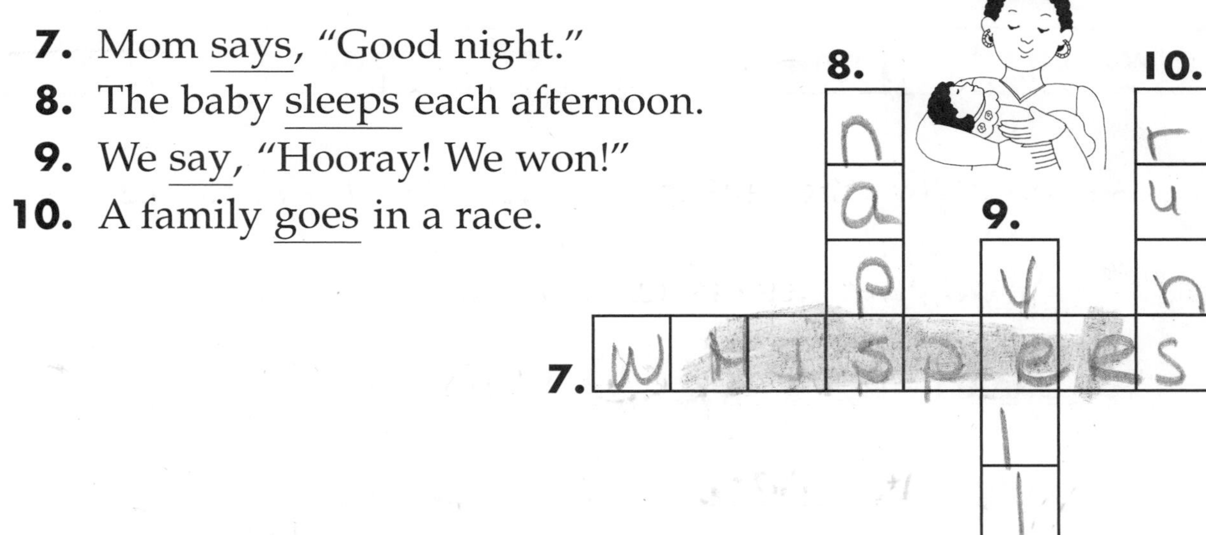

TRY THIS! Look up *sleep, go,* and *say* in your Thesaurus. Use the synonyms to write a sentence for each word. Then use the synonyms and the sentences to make up a word puzzle.

Name ____

Verbs That Tell About the Past

A. Underline the verb in each sentence that tells about the past. Write it on the line.

1. The bird landed on the grass. landed
2. It picked up a worm. picked
3. Two squirrels climbed up a tree. climbed
4. They stuffed their cheeks with acorns. stuffed
5. The squirrels played in the tree. played

B. Use a word from the box to complete each sentence.

watched	jumped	buzzed	leaped	crawled

6. A rabbit jumped on the grass.
7. A snake crawled near the rabbit.
8. Some bees buzzed around.
9. Frogs leaped by the pond.
10. The children watched the animals.

TRY THIS! Write two sentences about animals you have seen outside your home or school. Use verbs that tell about the past.

Name ______________________________

Adding *ed* to Verbs

A. Circle the ending that was added to each verb to tell about the past.

1. Kate milked the cows.

2. The cow pushed the calf gently.

3. Joshua lifted the bucket.

4. He dumped the hay on the ground.

5. The cows chewed on the food.

B. Change the verb in ( ) to tell about the past.

6. Kate **(pour)** poured water in a bucket.

7. Joshua **(fill)** filled another one.

8. The animals **(enjoy)** enjoyed the cool water.

9. The cows **(rest)** rested.

10. The children **(finish)** finished their chores.

TRY THIS! Write two sentences that tell about chores you have done. Use verbs that tell about the past in your sentences.

Name ______________________

Changing Verbs That End with *e*

A. Change the verb in ( ) to tell about the past.

1. The goat **(poke)** the fence. poked
2. It **(move)** quickly. moved
3. Gina **(close)** the gate. Closed
4. The children **(tease)** the animal. teased
5. The goat **(chase)** after them. Chased

B. Change the verb in each sentence to tell about the past. Write the new sentence.

6. Mom races outside.

Mom raced outside.

7. She places the goat in the pen.

She placed the goat in the pen.

8. Mom saves the day.

Mom saved the day.

TRY THIS! Write two sentences about a pet you own or an animal you have seen. Describe things the animal did. Use verbs that tell about the past in your sentences.

Name ______________________________

Extra Practice

A. Underline the verb in each sentence that tells about the past.

1. Lou visited the zoo.

2. The lions roared.

3. They stayed in their cage.

B. Circle the verb that tells about the past. Write it on the line.

4. The tigers **(walk, walked)** walked around.

5. A giraffe **(stretch, stretched)** stretched its neck.

6. The seals **(barked, bark)** barked.

C. Change the verb in ( ) to tell about the past. Write the new sentence.

7. Dylan **(face)** the monkey.

Dylan faced the monkey.

8. He **(smile)** at the monkey.

He smiled at the monkey.

Name ______________________________

Using a Dictionary Entry

bat 1. a wooden stick: *Bill hit the ball with the bat.* **2.** a kind of flying mammal that comes out at night: *Jill saw the bat fly down from the roof.*

beat 1. to hit: *I beat the drum.* **2.** to win: *I beat him in the race.*

bed 1. furniture made for sleeping: *Pascal rested on his bed.* **2.** bottom layer: *The beans were on a bed of lettuce.*

begin to start: *The alphabet begins with the letter A.*

best better than anything else: *Rosa is the best athlete.*

bold 1. very brave or confident: *The king was a bold leader.* **2.** bright, like a color: *She wore a bold blue dress.*

Use the dictionary entries to answer the questions.

1. What entry word comes after the word *beat*? bed

2. How many definitions are given for the word *bat*? 2

3. What is the meaning of the word *begin*? to Start

4. What does the word *beat* mean in this sentence? *Gina beat Tim at checkers.* to win

TRY THIS! Choose four words from the sample dictionary page. Use each word in a sentence.

Name ______________________________

The Verbs *Am, Is,* and *Are*

A. Read each sentence. Draw a line under the verb.

1. I am busy.

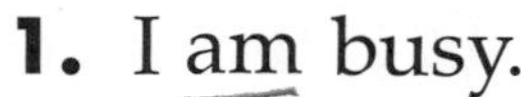

2. The telescope is on the tripod.
3. All of the clouds are gone.

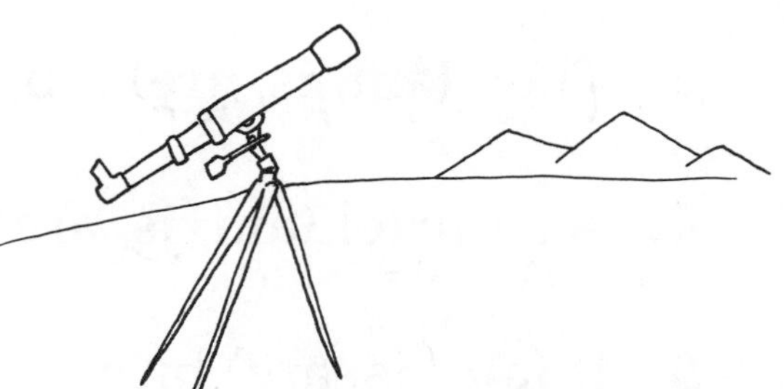

4. The stars are bright.
5. The night is pretty.

B. Write a word from the box to complete each sentence.

are	is	am

6. The sky ___is___ black.
7. Mom and I ___are___ outside.
8. The telescope ___is___ mine.
9. I ___am___ proud.
10. We ___are___ excited.

TRY THIS! Write three sentences that tell about the sky at night or during the day. Use the verbs *am, is,* and *are.*

Name ____

Using *Am, Is,* and *Are*

A. Circle the correct verb to finish each sentence.

1. I **(am, is, are)** in the park.
2. The birds **(am, is, are)** in the trees.
3. They **(am, is, are)** loud.
4. A squirrel **(am, is, are)** on the bench.
5. It **(am, is, are)** brown.

B. Write *am, is,* or *are* to complete each sentence.

6. Two rabbits are near.
7. The squirrel is quiet.
8. I am quiet, too.
9. The squirrel is very still.
10. Then the rabbits are gone.

TRY THIS! Write sentences about a park that you have visited. Tell about the people or animals you saw. Use the verbs *am, is,* and *are* in your sentences.

Name ______________________________

Using *Was* and *Were*

A. Circle the correct verb to finish each sentence.

1. Grace **(was, were)** on the boat.
2. Her parents **(was, were)** with her.
3. Many fish **(was, were)** in the water.
4. A seagull **(was, were)** overhead.
5. The sky **(was, were)** clear.

B. Write *was* or *were* to complete each sentence.

6. The weather was hot.
7. Soon Grace and her parents were on the shore.
8. Shells were everywhere.
9. Grace was happy.
10. Pretty shells were easy to find.

TRY THIS! Write two sentences about the last time you had time off from school. How did you feel? Where did you go? Use the verbs *was* and *were* in your sentences.

Name 

Extra Practice

A. Circle the verb in each sentence.

1. The snow is deep.
2. The trees are bare.
3. I am wet.

B. Write the correct verb to finish each sentence.

4. I **(am, is, are)** am cold.
5. A deer **(am, is, are)** is close.
6. Bushes **(am, is, are)** are between us.

C. Choose the verb that completes each sentence correctly. Write the new sentence.

7. The deer's eyes **(was, were)** bright. The deer's eyes were bright.
8. Its fur **(was, were)** brown. Its fur was brown.
9. Then the deer **(was, were)** gone. Then the deer was gone.
10. I **(was, were)** sad. I was sad.

Name ____________________

Taking a Test

A. Fill in the oval next to the correct answer.

1. Which answer choices should you read?
- ⬭ only the correct choice
- ⬭ half of the choices
- ⬬ all of the choices

2. When should you read the directions?
- ⬭ after the test
- ⬬ before the test
- ⬭ during the test

3. How should you plan your time on a test?
- ⬬ You should work very quickly.
- ⬭ You should do the easy items first.
- ⬭ You should spend time on the hard items first.

B. Fill in the oval that finishes the sentence correctly.

4. When you read an item, ____.
- ⬭ you should read quickly.
- ⬭ you should guess the answer right away.
- ⬬ you should find the important word or words.

TRY THIS! Work with a partner. Write short, fun quizzes for each other. Then do each other's quizzes. Did you follow the directions?

Name ______________________________

The Verbs *Has, Have,* and *Had*

A. Read each sentence. Underline the verb.

1. The plant has leaves.
2. Flowers have stems.
3. Last summer, I had a bunch of roses.
4. We had a flower garden.
5. Now we have a vegetable garden.

B. Write *has, have,* or *had* to complete each sentence.

6. The carrots have green tops now.
7. Yesterday, the garden had bugs.
8. Last spring, I had a watering can.
9. Today, I have a new can.
10. My brother has a new can, too.

TRY THIS! Write one sentence about something you have now. Write another sentence about something you had before. Use *have* and *had* in your sentences.

Name ______________________________

Using *Has, Have,* and *Had*

A. Circle the verb that correctly completes each sentence.

1. Animals **(has, have)** different body parts.
2. A giraffe **(has, have)** a long neck.
3. Elephants **(has, have)** trunks.
4. A zebra **(has, have)** stripes.
5. Last week, I saw a horse that **(have, had)** a mane.

B. Write *has, have,* or *had* to complete each sentence.

6. Turtles have shells.
7. A lion has sharp teeth.
8. A parrot has colorful feathers.
9. Last winter, I had a gerbil with a long tail.
10. Now I have a furry hamster.

TRY THIS! Think about three animals. Write a sentence about each animal that tells how it is different from the other two. Use the verbs *has, have,* and *had* in your sentences.

Name ____________________

Agreement with *Has, Have,* and *Had*

A. Use the verbs from the box to complete the sentences.

had	has	have

1. I have my new bathing suit on today.
2. Mom has one on now, too.
3. Yesterday I had fun in the pool.

B. Decide if *has, have,* or *had* is used correctly in each sentence. Write the incorrect sentences correctly.

4. We has a big pool.

We have a big pool.

5. We have races there each summer.

____

6. Now I had three ribbons.

Now I have three Ribbons.

TRY THIS! Write two sentences about something you own. Use *has, have,* and *had*.

Name ____________________

Extra Practice

A. Read each sentence. Underline the verb.

1. The cat has whiskers.
2. The kittens have closed eyes.
3. They had a nap earlier.

B. Circle the verb that completes each sentence.

4. The kittens **(has, have)** a soft bed.
5. The bed **(has, have)** a pillow.
6. Yesterday, the cat **(has, have, had)** a small ball.
7. Today, the kittens **(has, have, had)** the ball.

C. Decide if *has, have,* or *had* is used correctly in each sentence. Write the incorrect sentences correctly.

8. I has a cat, too.

   I have a cat, too

9. My cat has short fur.

   ____

10. Last summer, I have another cat.

    Last Summer, I had another Cat

Name ______________________________

Editing on a Computer

Follow the directions using a computer.

1. Type the following sentence:
Birds fly south.

2. Add the words *in the winter* so that the sentence says:
Birds fly south in the winter.

3. Add the word *Many* so that the sentence says:
Many birds fly south in the winter.

4. Move *in the winter* so that the sentence says:
in the winter Many birds fly south.

5. Make the letter *I* capital and the letter *M* lowercase so that the sentence says:
In the winter many birds fly south.

6. Add a comma so that the sentence says:
In the winter, many birds fly south.

TRY THIS! Use your computer skills to add, delete, or move text in a piece of your own writing.

Name ___________________________

What Is an Adjective?

A. Circle the adjective that describes the underlined noun in each sentence.

1. My big brother and I went riding.

2. I rode a black horse.

3. We took a new trail.

4. We spotted a brown bear.

5. What an exciting ride!

B. Write an adjective from the box to complete each sentence.

dusty	**cool**	**two**	**shady**	**sunny**

6. It was a hot dusty day.

7. The trail was dry and sunny.

8. Ben and I rode for two hours.

9. We rested in a shady spot.

TRY THIS! Write two sentences about what you might see if you went riding through the woods. Use adjectives in your sentences.

Name ____________________

Adjectives That Tell What Kind

A. Circle the adjective in each sentence. Write it on the line.

1. Look at your yellow pencil. yellow
2. Does it have a pointy tip? pointy
3. Is the other end flat? flat
4. Use your brown ruler. brown
5. Draw a straight line. straight

B. Write an adjective from the box to complete each sentence. Underline the noun the adjective describes.

round	silver	black	square	red

6. I need Square paper.
7. Do you have my black marker?
8. Your round eraser is under the table.
9. I can't find my red pencil.
10. Did you look in that silver can?

TRY THIS! Write three sentences about items you use in art class. Use adjectives that tell about color and shape.

Name ______________________________

Writing Longer Sentences

A. Read each sentence. Circle the adjectives that tell about the underlined noun.

1. Here is a round blue button.

2. I found it on the big red chair.

3. It was under the square yellow pillow.

4. I'll check my big white shirt.

B. Add adjectives to describe the nouns in each sentence. Write the new sentence.

5. I have a coat.

I have a heavy black coat.

6. My coat has pockets.

My coat hase two big pockets

7. It has buttons.

It has big red buttons

TRY THIS! Write a sentence about something you are wearing. Then rewrite the sentence as many times as you can. Add a new adjective each time.

Name ___________________________________

Extra Practice

A. Underline the adjective in each sentence. Circle the noun it describes.

1. How dark the woods are today!

2. The tall trees block the sunlight.

3. The leaves are green.

B. Write an adjective from the box to complete each sentence.

pointy	black	gray

4. Have you ever seen a gray wolf?

5. Its tail has a black tip.

6. What sharp pointy fangs it has!

C. Add adjectives to describe the noun in each sentence. Write the new sentence.

7. Do you see the owl?

Do you see the gray owl?

8. It is on the tree.

It is on the tall tree.

Name ____________________

Using a Thesaurus

A. Read the entry for *nice* in your Thesaurus on pages 494–498. Write a synonym for *nice* that best completes each sentence.

1. A cool breeze is ____________ on a hot day.

2. We saw a ____________ yellow bird on the feeder.

3. Meg is a ____________ person, so she has many friends.

4. Thank you for the ____________ gift.

5. Grandma had a ____________ visit with the children.

B. Read the entry for *eat* in your Thesaurus on pages 494–498. Write a synonym for eat that best completes each sentence.

6. My sister will ____________ spaghetti for the first time tonight.

7. After school Carrie and Ted ____________ on carrots.

8. My dogs always ____________ their food quickly.

TRY THIS! Write three sentences that use *good* to describe someone or something. Then rewrite each sentence using a synonym for *good*. Use your Thesaurus.

Name ______________________________

Words That Tell About the Senses

A. Draw a line from the underlined word in Column A to the sense that it tells about in Column B.

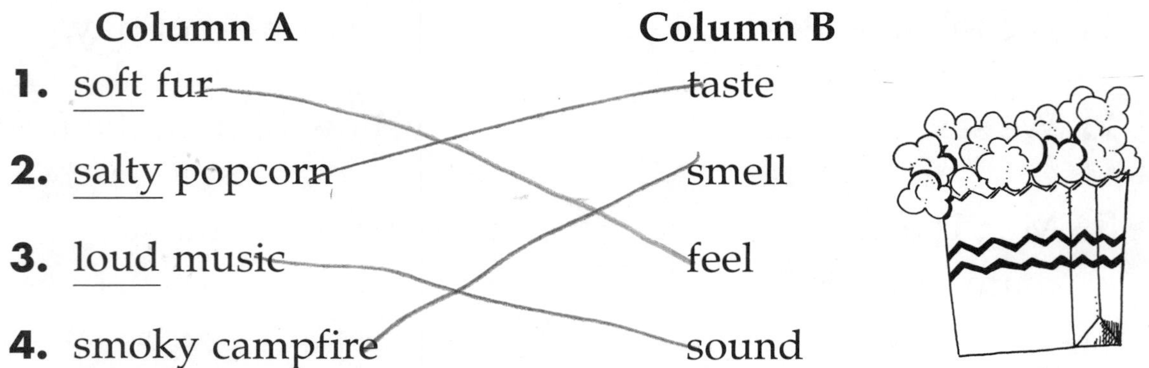

Column A	Column B
1. soft fur	taste
2. salty popcorn	smell
3. loud music	feel
4. smoky campfire	sound

B. Write a word from the box to complete each sentence.

spicy	quiet	warm	slippery	tasty	icy

5. It is a ___quiet___ day.

6. An ___icy___ wind is blowing.

7. I walk up the ___Slippery___ hill to my house.

8. It is ___warm___ in the house.

9. I smell something ___Spicy___.

10. Dad is baking ___tasty___ muffins.

TRY THIS! Write two sentences about your favorite foods. Use adjectives that tell about the senses in your sentences.

Name ____________________

Adjectives for Taste, Smell, Feel, and Sound

A. Underline the adjective in each sentence. Write it on the line.

1. It's a hot afternoon at the beach. hot
2. Noisy gulls look for food. noisy
3. A man races across the burning sand. burning
4. This seaweed has a fishy smell. fishy
5. How salty the air is today! salty

B. Write a word from the box to complete each sentence.

shrill	sticky	fruity	slippery	fresh

6. Don't climb on the slippery rocks.
7. A lifeguard's shrill whistle warns swimmers.
8. This sunscreen is sticky!
9. A fresh breeze blows across the beach.
10. A child enjoys a fruity ice cone.

TRY THIS! Write two sentences about a summer day at the beach, lake, or pool. Use adjectives for taste, feel, sound, and smell.

Name ________________________________

Using Synonyms in Writing

A. Read each group of words. Underline the two synonyms.

1. hot	steaming	chunky
2. chilly	smooth	freezing
3. wet	crunchy	soggy
4. narrow	uneven	rough
5. soft	furry	hard

B. Circle the more exact adjective to finish each sentence. Write the new sentence.

6. Feel the **(velvety, soft)** moss on this rock.

Feel the soft moss on this rock.

7. Walk slowly along this **(uneven, bumpy)** path.

Walk slowly along this uneven path.

8. Rain made the rocks **(slippery, wet)**.

Rain made the rocks slippery

TRY THIS! Choose one thing you might hear, smell, feel, or see in the woods. Then write four sentences to describe it. Use exact adjectives in your sentences.

Name ______________________________

Words for Size and Number

A. Write a word from the box to finish each sentence.

seven	little	twenty	many	big

1. I read a ____________ book with my mother.
2. The book has ____________ pages.
3. It is about a ____________ girl named Lucy.
4. She is ____________ years old.
5. She has ____________ friends.

B. Circle the adjectives that tell size or number.

6. Lucy lives on a huge farm.
7. She has some animals.
8. Five horses live in a stable.
9. Her goat just had three kids.
10. The kids are small.

TRY THIS! Write sentences about a book you read. Describe the characters and the story. Use adjectives that tell size and number.

Name ____

Adjectives That Tell How Many

A. Write a word from the box to finish each sentence.

four	few	some	many	five

1. My neighbor is _________ years old.
2. She has _________ tea parties.
3. Every day she puts out four plates and _________ cups.
4. She has _________ play food.
5. I sit on the floor because there are _________ chairs.

B. Fill in each blank with an adjective that tells how many.

6. Carrie always invites ______________ stuffed animals.
7. Her mother lets her have ______________ cookies.
8. She puts ______________ cookie on each plate.
9. After the party, she cleans ______________ of the dishes.
10. She will have another party in ______________ days.

TRY THIS! Write two sentences about a snack you enjoy. Use adjectives that tell how many.

Name ______________________________

Using *a* and *an*

A. Write *a* or *an* to complete each sentence.

1. There is _____ library in Don's town.
2. _____ older woman works there.
3. She shows Don _____ special shelf.
4. Don sees _____ unusual book.
5. There is _____ river on the cover.

B. Decide if *a* or *an* is used correctly in each sentence. Write the incorrect sentences correctly.

6. Inside the book is a animal. ______________________________

____

7. The animal has a furry body. ______________________________

____

8. It is called a otter. ______________________________

____

TRY THIS! Write two nouns that begin with a consonant. Then write two nouns that begin with a vowel. Write sentences using these words. Be sure to use *a* and *an* correctly.

Name ______________________________

Extra Practice

A. Circle the words that tell size or number.

1. Angel made her room into a large zoo.
2. She used many stuffed animals.
3. She had six pens.
4. She used her bed for a small pen.

B. In each sentence, write an adjective that tells how many.

5. ______________ bears were on her bed.

6. ______________ pens had monkeys in them.

7. Angel had only ______________ zebra.

C. Decide if *a* or *an* is used correctly in each sentence. Write the incorrect sentences correctly.

8. Two friends took a look at the zoo. ______________

____

9. They thought it was a interesting idea. ______________

____

10. Kira wanted to borrow an bear. ______________

____

Name ______________________________

Using Spell-Check

Read the sentences. The misspelled words are underlined. Look at the choices in spell-check. Circle the word you would choose.

1. Jessie is a grat athlete.

   Replace with: great grape grated

2. She is good at sockr.

   Replace with: sock soccer soaker

3. It is her favorit sport.

   Replace with: favor favorite fantastic

4. She goes to camp in the sumer.

   Replace with: sum something summer

5. They play gaimes each day.

   Replace with: gems gains games

6. This year her taem won the camp award.

   Replace with: team tam meat

TRY THIS! Type a story from your portfolio on a computer. Use the spell-check program to check it for misspelled words. Correct each one.

Name ____________________

Words That Compare

A. Underline the adjectives that compare.

1. We just had the warmest summer ever.
2. August was warmer than it was last year.
3. We stayed in the pool longer today than yesterday.
4. Sue can swim faster than I can.
5. Melinda is the fastest swimmer of all.

B. Write an adjective from the box to finish each sentence.

coldest	cooler	brighter	longer	highest

6. The sun seems ____________ in the spring and summer.
7. The sun is ____________ in the sky in the summer.
8. Fall air is ____________ in the evening than in the afternoon.
9. Winter is the ____________ season of all.
10. It seems to last ____________ than the other seasons.

TRY THIS! Write two sentences that tell how seasons are different. Use adjectives that compare.

Name ______________________________

Adding *er* and *est*

A. Circle the ending that was added to each adjective that compares. Then write whether it compares two things or more than two things.

1. This is the tallest redwood tree! ____________

2. Is it older than the tree next to it? ____________

3. It makes the longest shadow of all. ____________

4. This tree has a thicker bark than that one. ____________

5. The needles are shorter than my finger! ____________

B. Circle the correct form of the adjective in ( ) to finish each sentence.

6. A redwood has **(softer, softest)** wood than an elm tree.

7. Are redwood seeds the **(smaller, smallest)** of all?

8. Which tree has **(darker, darkest)** bark than this one?

9. This pine tree has the **(sharper, sharpest)** needles of all.

10. Our pine tree has **(greener, greenest)** needles than this one.

TRY THIS! Draw pictures of three trees. Write sentences telling how they are different. Use adjectives with *er* and *est*.

Name ______________________________

Writing to Compare

A. Add *er* or *est* to a word from the box to finish each sentence.

1. Are giraffes the ______________ animals of all?

2. Does a frog have ______________ skin than a toad?

3. Does an alligator have a ______________ snout than a crocodile?

B. Read each sentence pair. Then add *er* or *est* to the underlined word to complete the second sentence.

4. Cheetahs, lions, and zebras are fast.

   Cheetahs are the ______________ runners of all.

5. Ostriches have long necks.

   Giraffes have ______________ necks than ostriches.

6. Turtles are slow animals.

   Snails are even ______________ than turtles.

TRY THIS! Write three questions that compare animals. Use adjectives with *er* and *est*.

Name ______________________________

Extra Practice

A. Underline the adjectives that compare.

1. We are putting on the greatest puppet show ever.
2. Mary made the smallest puppet of all!
3. Steven's puppet has longer hair than mine.
4. Your puppet has fewer buttons than his.

B. Underline the adjectives that compare two nouns. Circle the adjectives that compare more than two nouns.

5. My puppet has the brightest smile of all.
6. Ann wants a smaller part than Luis.
7. Luis is bolder than she is.

C. Add *er* or *est* to a word from the box to finish each sentence.

loud	soft	quiet

8. She has the ________________ voice in our class.

9. Ann is ________________ than everyone else.

10. Ann did such a good job that her puppet got the

________________ laughs of all.

Name ______________________________

Using Pictographs and Bar Graphs

Use the information on the pictograph and the bar graph to answer the questions.

Favorite Ice Cream	
Chocolate	🍦 🍦 🍦 🍦
Strawberry	🍦 🍦 🍦
Vanilla	🍦 🍦 🍦 🍦 🍦
Key: 🍦 = 1 vote	

Favorite Ice Cream						
Chocolate	■	■	■	■		
Strawberry	■	■	■			
Vanilla	■	■	■	■	■	
	1	**2**	**3**	**4**	**5**	**6**

1. How many children's votes are shown on each graph?

____

2. Did more children choose chocolate or vanilla?

____

3. Which flavor did only three children choose?

____

4. How many children voted for chocolate?

____

TRY THIS! Write directions that explain how to use one of the graphs above.

Name ______________________________

The Verbs *Come, Run,* and *Give*

A. Circle the correct verb in ( ) to complete each sentence.

1. I **(come, comes)** to the same cabin each summer.
2. My mother **(run, runs)** around the lake each morning.
3. Sometimes I **(run, runs)** with her.
4. My dog Sparky **(come, comes)**, too.
5. Then my mother **(give, gives)** me breakfast.

B. Write the correct form of *come, run,* or *give* to complete each sentence.

6. After breakfast, I ____________ back to the lake.
7. I ____________ over to my stepfather's boat.
8. He ____________ me a fishing lesson.
9. Then he ____________ me some time to play in the water.
10. I always ____________ to my special place.

TRY THIS! Write two sentences about a place that is special to you. Use the verbs *come, run,* and *give* in your sentences.

Name ______________________________

Using *Come, Run,* and *Give*

A. Change the verb in ( ) to tell about the past.

1. I **(come)** __________ to school early.

2. I **(run)** __________ from the bus stop.

3. I **(give)** __________ my friend help before class.

4. Jake **(gives)** __________ a report.

5. He **(comes)** __________ early to help me, too.

B. Underline the correct verb in ( ) to complete each sentence.

6. Last year Jake **(gives, gave)** me a special birthday card.

7. Now I **(come, came)** to his house each day.

8. I **(run, ran)** there after school.

9. I **(give, gave)** him his favorite book last month.

10. Now he **(come, comes)** to my house on the weekends.

TRY THIS! Write two sentences about a person who is special to you. What things do you do together? Use the past tense and present tense of the verbs *come, run,* and *give* in your sentences.

Name ____

Joining Sentences

A. Use a comma to correct each sentence.

1. It is Parents' Day at school and the auditorium is full.

2. The principal gives a speech and everyone listens.

3. He welcomes parents and they smile at him.

4. The principal thanks the parents and he ends his speech.

5. The children find their parents and they lead them to the classrooms.

B. Use *and* to join the sentences. Remember to use a comma before *and*. Write the new sentence.

6. Mandy's mom is a police officer. She speaks to Mr. Tan's class. ___________________________________

____

7. Mandy is proud. She gives her mother a hug.

____

TRY THIS! Write two sentences that tell about what you want to do when you grow up. Then combine the two sentences to make one sentence.

Name ____

Extra Practice

A. Circle the correct verb in ( ) to complete each sentence.

1. We **(come, comes)** to this museum each year.

2. I **(run, runs)** to catch up to Mike and Tony.

3. Our teacher **(give, gives)** us a paper.

B. Change the verb in ( ) to tell about the past.

4. The paper **(gives)** __________ dinosaur facts.

5. We **(come)** __________ to the dinosaur room.

6. A tiny model dinosaur **(runs)** __________ through a maze.

7. A tour guide **(gives)** __________ us a tour.

C. Use *and* to join the sentences. Remember to use a comma before *and*.

8. The museum was big. I couldn't see everything.

____

9. I loved everything I saw. I want to go back.

____

Name ______________________________

Using a Newspaper

Read the newspaper story. Use it to answer each question below.

Student Starts Club
by *Shennell Barnes*

In September James Terry started a club at Prescott Elementary School. It's called the Clean School Club. He started it because he wanted to have a clean playground at school. At first he was the only member. Then he invited classmates to help him. Now the club has fifty members.

1. Who is this article about? ______________________________

2. What did he do? ______________________________

____

3. Where did James Terry start his club? ______________________________

____

4. When did he start the club? ______________________________

5. Why did James start the club? ______________________________

____

TRY THIS! Write a newspaper story about something exciting that happened to you. Remember to answer the questions *who, what, when, where,* and *why* in your story.

Name ___________________________________

The Verbs *Go, Do,* and *See*

A. Use a word from the box to complete each sentence.

did	see	go	do	saw

1. I _______ to the library on Saturdays with my father.

2. We _______ interesting things.

3. We _______ a funny puppet show last month.

4. Sometimes I _______ my homework there.

5. Last Saturday, I _______ my whole science project.

B. Circle the correct verb in ( ) to complete each sentence.

6. One time I **(sees, saw)** an exciting video.

7. It was about a man who **(go, goes)** to different countries.

8. He **(did, do)** a dangerous thing to save a tiger cub.

9. Someone **(saw, see)** the cub trapped on a cliff.

10. The man **(go, went)** to the cliff and set the cub free.

TRY THIS! Write three sentences about characters in your favorite book or video. Use the verbs *go, do* and *see* in your sentences.

Name ______________________________

Using *Go, Do,* and *See*

A. Change the verb in ( ) to tell about the past.

1. I **(go)** __________ to a dance recital.
2. I **(see)** __________ beautiful ballerinas.
3. They **(do)** __________ graceful turns.
4. One dancer **(do)** __________ a hard jump.
5. I **(see)** __________ him smile when he landed.

B. Circle the correct verb to finish each sentence.

6. I **(go, went)** to dance class tomorrow.
7. Last week I **(go, went)** for the first time.
8. Dancers must **(do, did)** a lot of practicing.
9. I practice often since I **(see, saw)** the dancers.
10. I hope I **(do, did)** beautiful dances like them one day.

TRY THIS! Write three sentences that use *go, do,* and *see.* Trade papers with a classmate. Write your classmate's sentences using verbs that tell about the past.

Name ____________________

Commas in Place Names and Dates

A. Add commas to write the dates and the names of places correctly.

(1) May 4 2001 Dear Beth, I like being in **(2)** Seattle Washington. It rains more than in **(3)** Austin Texas. We will be home soon. Amy	Beth Pardie 935 West End Avenue **(4)** Baltimore Maryland 21228

B. Fill in the chart with the dates and the names of places.

	When (date)	Where (place name)
The day you were born	**5.**	**6.**
A trip you went on	**7.**	**8.**
A person you visited	**9.**	**10.**

TRY THIS! Use the chart to write sentences about the day you were born, a special trip, and a special visit. Remember to use commas.

Name ___________________________________

Extra Practice

A. Write a word from the box to complete each sentence.

sees	goes	do

1. My sister __________ to the ballet often.
2. She __________ dancers leaping and spinning.
3. The dancers __________ hard moves.

B. Circle the correct verb in each sentence.

4. Sometimes she **(does, did)** the same steps as the dancers.
5. I **(go, went)** to a ballet class with my sister last month.
6. She still **(goes, went)** to class to get better.

C. Rewrite the sentences. Put commas in the dates and names of places.

7. We live in Kansas City Missouri.

____

8. We saw a ballet on October 31 2003.

____

Name ______________________________

Using a Map

Read the map. Use it to answer each question below.

1. How many traffic lights are there? ______________

2. What is next to the shoe store? ______________

3. Who lives across the street from the school? ______________

4. On what street is Sue's house? ______________

5. How would Brent walk to Eric's house? ______________

____

TRY THIS! Make a simple map of your block. Draw the streets. Make a square for each building or house. Label each street and three buildings or houses.

Name ______________________________

What Is a Helping Verb?

A. Underline the helping verb in each sentence. Then circle the verb it helps.

1. Yesterday our class had decided to make papier-mâché dinosaurs.

2. Today Charles has gathered the supplies.

3. He has placed them on the table.

4. I have passed newspaper to my classmates.

B. Write the correct helping verb to finish each sentence.

5. Last night I **(has, had)** __________ planned my dinosaur.

6. Now I **(have, had)** __________ shaped the newspaper into a dinosaur.

7. We **(has, have)** __________ dipped newspaper strips into the glue.

8. Ms. Scott **(has, have)** __________ helped me add the strips onto my dinosaur.

TRY THIS! Write three sentences about an art project or drawing you have done. Tell the steps you took to make it. Use helping verbs in your sentences.

Name ______________________________

Using *Has, Have,* and *Had*

A. Read each sentence. Fill in each blank with *have* or *has.*

1. Richie __________ picked up the camera today.

2. Mom __________ told him not to touch it.

3. Now she __________ put it on a high shelf.

4. Sandy and I __________ used it.

5. We __________ followed directions.

B. Underline the correct helping verb to finish each sentence.

6. I **(have, has)** used a camera before.

7. Last week Dad **(have, had)** shown me how.

8. Yesterday we **(had, has)** developed the film.

9. Now I **(have, has)** seen all the pictures.

10. Dad **(have, has)** taken them to show Mom.

TRY THIS! Write three sentences about using a camera or having your picture taken. Use helping verbs in your sentences.

Name ____________________

Keeping to One Main Idea

A. Read the paragraph. Cross out two sentences that do not keep to the main idea.

1. I have drawn a picture. It is red, blue, yellow, and green. My picture shows flowers and fruit. Pears are my favorite fruit to eat. In the summer, I like to eat grapes. It took me only one day to draw the picture.

B. Underline the main idea in each paragraph. Cross out the sentence that does not tell about the main idea.

2. I found a fun room at the Baker Art Museum last week. A woman told me about the new children's room. She wore a red dress and black shoes. The room had pretty pictures that I could touch. An artist was there, too. He answered my questions about painting.

3. Making papier-mâché animals is easy. First, bend newspaper into the shape of an animal. My father loves to read the newspaper. Next, soak newspaper strips in glue and water. Then, wrap the strips around your animal shape. Last, paint your animal when it is all dry.

TRY THIS! Write four sentences about a painting or a picture you like. Use a main idea sentence and detail sentences. Keep to one main idea.

Name ____

Extra Practice

A. Underline the helping verb in each sentence. Then circle the verb it helps.

1. Jill has worked hard on her painting.

2. She has entered it in the art show.

3. She had won second place in the show last year.

4. Her brother Mark has helped her carry the painting.

B. Write *has* or *have* to make each sentence correct.

5. Mark __________ bought two tickets to the show.

6. He __________ invited a friend.

7. Today they __________ used the tickets.

C. Underline the main idea. Cross out the sentence that does not tell about the main idea.

8. Mark liked the art show. He arrived early. Then he walked around and looked closely at each painting. It was raining outside. Mark liked the colorful paintings best. He also liked the drawings of animals.

Name ____________________

Using Computer Graphics

On your computer, type a piece of writing from your Writing Portfolio. Then use the tips below to add graphics to your page.

1. Use different kinds of type.

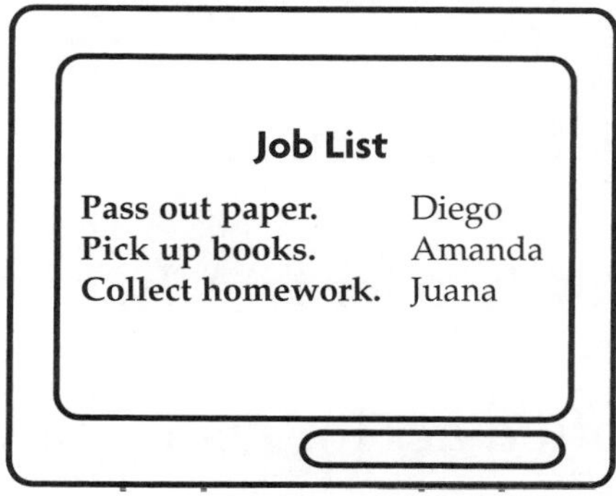

2. Add two pictures to your page.

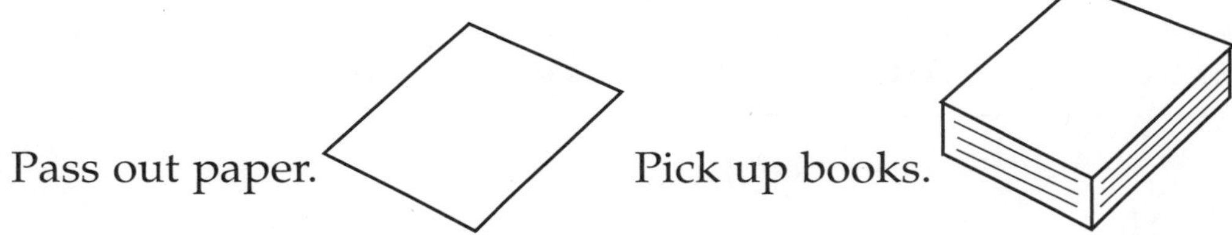

3. Place a border around your page.

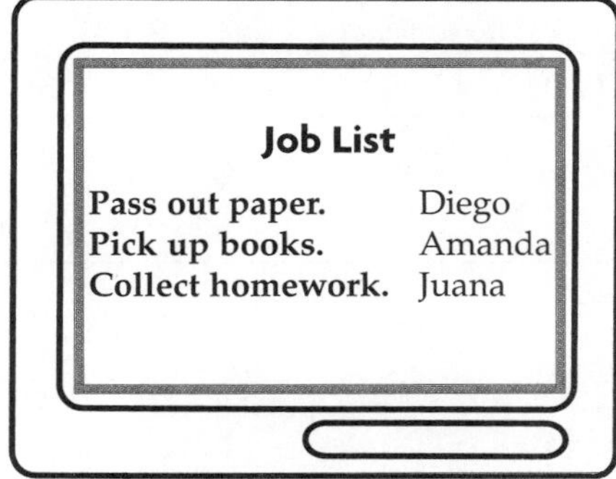

TRY THIS! Write directions that explain how you added graphics to your piece of writing. Add the directions to your Writing Portfolio.

Name ____

What Is an Adverb?

A. Underline the adverb in each sentence.

1. Jason arrives early at the auditorium.

2. He walks quickly to the stage.

3. Ally waits quietly for Trina.

4. Trina walks slowly over to Ally.

5. The children often act in school plays.

B. Write an adverb from the box to complete each sentence.

carefully	loudly	eagerly	happily	always

6. Bart ____________________ tries out for the lead.

7. His mother ____________________ helps him practice.

8. Children laugh ____________________ at the funny lines.

9. Ming climbs ____________________ up the ladder.

10. She smiles ____________________ as she paints the scenery.

TRY THIS! Write two sentences about a project you have done with your class or with a partner. Be sure to include lively adverbs.

Name ______________________________

Using Adverbs

A. Decide whether each adverb from the box tells *how, when,* or *where*. Write it on the chart.

inside	sometimes	slowly
never	above	sadly

Tells *How*	Tells *When*	Tells *Where*
1. ____________	**3.** ____________	**5.** ____________
2. ____________	**4.** ____________	**6.** ____________

B. Circle the adverb in each sentence. Write whether it tells *how, when,* or *where*.

7. The workbench downstairs has many tools. ____________

8. Yesterday, my dad and I worked on the set for the play. ____________

9. He used the hammer carefully. ____________

10. We often build things together. ____________

TRY THIS! Write four sentences to describe something you do when school is out. Be sure to use adverbs that tell *how, when,* and *where*. Draw a picture to go with the sentences.

Name ____

Writing with Adverbs

A. Circle the adverb that answers the question.

1. **How?** The lights shone **(brightly, here)**.
2. **Where?** Lisa stood **(near, proudly)** the stage.
3. **How?** She cleared her throat **(softly, today)**.
4. **When?** Lisa **(often, quickly)** gets shy in front of people.
5. **When?** The feeling **(slowly, soon)** goes away.

B. Add an adverb that answers the question in ( ). Write the new sentence.

6. Then Lisa walked onstage. **(How?)**

____

7. Everyone was quiet. **(Where?)**

____

8. She said her lines. **(How?)**

____

TRY THIS! Change your sentences from Part B. Write new sentences using different adverbs. Think of adverbs that mean the opposite of the adverb you choose.

Name ____________________

Extra Practice

A. Circle the adverb in each sentence.

1. The rest of the play went smoothly.
2. The students perform well.
3. They feel proud of themselves today.

B. Write the adverb in each sentence. Then write *how, when,* or *where* for each adverb.

4. Soon the show was over. ____________________
5. The actors changed out of the costumes quickly. ____________________
6. Then they went outside to see their families. ____________________

C. Add an adverb to each sentence to give more details. Write the new sentence.

7. Lisa's grandmother was waiting.

____

8. Her grandmother hugged her.

____

Name ____________________

Using the Library

A. Write *fiction* or *nonfiction* to tell where you would find each book in the library.

1. *The Stories Huey Tells* by Ann Cameron ____________

2. *510 Math Puzzles for Your Brain* by Tom Harris ____________

3. *Cloudy With a Chance of Meatballs* by Judi Barrett ____________

4. *590 Spooky Spiders* by Jackie Thiel ____________

5. *570 Evergreen Trees* by Robert Sherman ____________

6. *Frog and Toad Are Friends* by Arnold Lobel ____________

B. Look at the books in items 1–6.

7. Write the fiction book titles in ABC order by the author's last name. ____________

____

Name ____

Nouns and Pronouns Together

A. Underline the pronoun in each sentence.

1. They have a good breakfast each morning.

2. Today she eats oatmeal.

3. It is delicious.

4. He has cereal and fruit.

5. She tastes his breakfast.

6. They like to share.

B. Write a pronoun from the box to complete each sentence.

she	**They**	**He**	**It**

7. __________ finishes his cereal first.

8. __________ is his favorite breakfast.

9. Then __________ finishes her oatmeal.

10. __________ clean the dishes together.

TRY THIS! Write three sentences about your favorite meal of the day. What do you eat? Who eats with you? Use pronouns in your sentences.

Name ____________________

Noun-Pronoun Agreement

A. Circle the pronoun that could replace the underlined noun in each sentence.

1. Charles likes to go camping. **(She, He)**

2. Denise enjoys camping, too. **(It, She)**

3. The children like camping because it teaches them about nature. **(it, they)**

B. Write the pronoun that agrees with the underlined noun or nouns in each set of sentences.

4. The campground is large.

   ________ is twenty miles wide.

5. Charles knows this campground well.

   ________ first came here when he was five.

6. Charles and Denise set up their tent.

   ________ finish quickly.

TRY THIS! Write three sentences about something your friends like to do. Use a pronoun in each sentence.

Name ____________________

Word Order for Pronouns

A. Write the correct words in ( ) to complete each sentence.

1. **(I and Brad, Brad and I)** like to read. ____________________

2. Mom reads to **(Brad and me, me and Brad)** each night. ____________________

3. **(Dad and I, I and Dad)** tell great stories. ____________________

B. Put the underlined words in the correct order. Write the new sentence.

4. I and my brother went to the library.

____

5. Brad looked at books with me and the librarian.

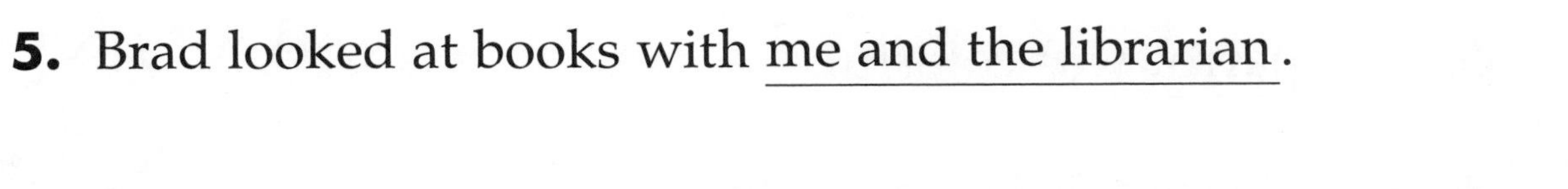

____

6. I and Brad found a book about the Grand Canyon.

____

TRY THIS! Write two sentences about something you and your friends do after school. Use at least one pronoun in each sentence.

Name ______________________________

Extra Practice

A. Underline the pronoun in each sentence. Then find and circle it in the puzzle. Words can go up, down, across, or backwards.

O	B	S	C
N	E	H	N
T	H	E	Y
P	T	I	L

1. He went to camp for the first time.
2. It was a lonely place.
3. Then she became his first friend.
4. They had lots of fun.

B. Write the pronoun that agrees with the underlined noun in each set of sentences.

5. Todd joined the art class at camp.

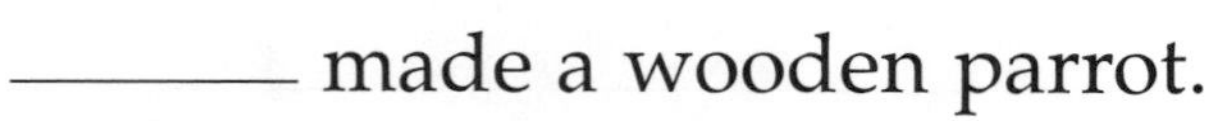

_______ made a wooden parrot.

6. The parrot was colorful.

_______ had yellow and blue wings.

7. Tammy sat next to Todd.

_______ worked on a drawing of a kitten.

Name ______________________________

Using a Telephone Book

Use the page from a telephone book to answer each question.

Samuels - Suarez

SAMUELS, Cindy	**SMITH, K.**
34 West St. 555-0112	5 Thomas Circle 555-0120
SANBORN, George	**SMITH, Shawna**
62 Fifth Ave. 555-0122	267 Arcadia Place 555-0115
SANTOS, Lauren	**STANTON, Len**
19 Withers Ave. 555-0173	315 Rose Lane 555-0123
SEARLE, Lee	**SUAREZ, N.**
82 Park St. 555-0164	78 Branch St. 555-0103

1. What is Lee Searle's phone number? ______________________
2. Who else could be on this page—Monica Stevens, Stanley Thomas, or John Swift? ______________________
3. Who lives at 19 Withers Ave? ______________________
4. Where would Tanisha Scard go on this page?

   ____
5. Why are the guide words for this page Samuels - Suarez?

   ____

TRY THIS! Make your own telephone book. Write the names and phone numbers of ten people you know. Then put the names in ABC order.

Name ______________________________

Subject-Verb Agreement

A. Write the correct verb to complete each sentence.

1. The baby kangaroo **(ride, rides)** in the pouch. __________
2. He **(peeks, peek)** out. __________
3. The mother kangaroo **(hops, hop)** down the trail. __________
4. Then she **(stop, stops)** to get food. __________
5. She **(eat, eats)** quickly. __________

B. Use a word from the box to complete each sentence.

swims	look	swing	watch	naps

6. Jack and Mona __________ the kangaroos.
7. Then the children __________ at other animals.
8. A polar bear __________ in the cool water.
9. A goat __________ under a tree.
10. The monkeys __________ from branch to branch.

TRY THIS! Write three sentences about things that zoo animals do. Underline the verbs.

Name ____

Changing *y* to *i*

A. Circle the correct form of the verb.

1. Theresa **(hurries, hurrys)** to the lake.
2. She **(carrys, carries)** a sack.
3. She (**tries, trys)** to climb into the boat.
4. Fred **(scurrys, scurries)** behind her.
5. A bird **(flys, flies)** onto the boat.

B. Write the correct form of the verb in ( ).

6. Another bird **(copy)** ________________ the first bird and lands on the boat.
7. The boat **(carry)** ________________ Theresa and Fred.
8. Fred **(study)** ________________ the sky.
9. Theresa **(spy)** ________________ a fish in the water.
10. She **(try)** ________________ to guess what kind it is.

TRY THIS! Use the following words in sentences that tell about one: *try, fry,* and *carry*. Draw a picture for each sentence.

Name ______________________________

Writing Contractions

can't	shouldn't	aren't	doesn't	didn't

A. Write a contraction from the box for the underlined words.

1. Steve does not have an umbrella. ____________

2. He should not play in the rain. ____________

3. The others are not outside. ____________

4. They did not bring umbrellas. ____________

5. Steve cannot wait to go out. ____________

B. Write a contraction for the underlined words.

6. The rain is not stopping. ____________

7. They were not ready for this. ____________

8. The wind has not stopped blowing. ____________

9. Lisa cannot walk home in the storm. ____________

10. They have not been outside all day. ____________

TRY THIS! Write three sentences about things you do not do when there is bad weather. Use contractions in your sentences.

Name ____________________

Extra Practice

A. Circle the correct verb to complete each sentence.

1. Tiana and her friends **(waits, wait)** with her mom.
2. Mom **(point, points)** to the sky diver.
3. The diver **(glides, glide)** through the sky.
4. Soon the parachute **(open, opens)** wide.

B. Write the correct form of the verb in ( ) on the line.

5. The diver **(fly)** ____________ through the sky.
6. She **(carry)** ____________ a small banner.
7. Tiana **(try)** ____________ to read the banner.

C. Write a contraction for the underlined words.

8. She cannot read the banner yet. 
9. She does not know it is for her. 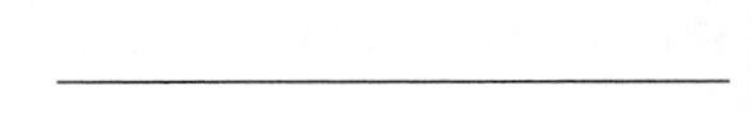
10. Her party was not supposed to start until tomorrow. ____________

Name ____________________

Using an Atlas

Use the map of New Mexico to answer the questions.

1. What is the capital of New Mexico? ____________________

2. Name another city in New Mexico. ____________________

3. What river is Albuquerque near? ____________________

4. Name a mountain range. ____________________

5. Name a national park. ____________________

TRY THIS! Work with a partner. Use the map to write directions for going from one place to another.

Name ____________________

Fixing "And Then" Sentences

Write each paragraph using time-order words.

1. On Saturday my mother and I made tacos. She heated up beans and then we got lettuce, tomatoes, and cheese and then we put all the food in the taco shells.

____

____

____

2. Jay got a cold last weekend. His throat was sore and then he started to cough and then he took medicine and then he took a nap.

____

____

____

TRY THIS! Write a paragraph about something you did one weekend. Use time-order words in your paragraph.

Name ______________________________

Writing Longer Sentences

Combine each set of sentences to make one longer sentence. Write the new sentence.

1. The students are ready for the tour.
The teachers are ready for the tour.

____

____

2. They point at the radio station.
They stare at the radio station.

____

3. The building is tall.
The building is shiny.

____

4. They visit the studio.
They take pictures of the studio.

____

____

TRY THIS! Write three short sentences about an adventure you have had. Then combine the sentences into one.

Name ____________________

Using a Series Comma

A. Underline the sentence in each pair that is written correctly.

1. Our class will create write, and perform skits.
   Our class will create, write, and perform skits.

2. Groups will have two, three, or four people.
   Groups will have two, three or four people.

3. The skits can be funny sad real, or made-up.
   The skits can be funny, sad, real, or made-up.

4. Groups can borrow, make or bring costumes.
   Groups can borrow, make, or bring costumes.

B. Write each sentence correctly.

5. Jamal Reese and Tammy worked in a group.

____

____

6. Their skit was about an owl a chicken and a parrot.

____

____

TRY THIS! Write three sentences about a project you have worked on with classmates. Use a list in each sentence.

Name ____________________

Extra Practice

A. Write the sentences using time-order words.

1. The mother bird lays eggs and then she sits on them. And then the eggs hatch.

____

____

B. Combine each set of sentences to make one longer sentence.

2. Robins have red feathers. Robins have orange feathers.

____

3. Robins eat insects. Robins eat fruit.

____

C. Write the sentence correctly.

4. Birds build nests with twigs grass and mud.

____

____

Name ____________________

Suffixes

A. Read each sentence. Add *-ful* or *-less* to complete the underlined word.

1. I am not afraid of that harm________ bug.
2. A bee can be harm________.
3. Be care________ not to get a bee sting.
4. If you are care________, the bee might sting you.

B. Use words from the box to complete the sentences.

careful	useless	colorful	thoughtful

5. Mom was ________________ to buy me the book.
6. I will be very ________________ with it.
7. If it rips, it will be ________________.
8. The book is filled with ________________ pictures.

TRY THIS! Write sentences using each of the following words: *fearless, fearful, restful, restless.* Draw a picture to go with each sentence.

Name ____________________

Spelling Words That Sound Alike

A. Use the words from the box to complete the sentences.

their	**they're**	**there**

1. My friends left a note for me ________.
2. It said ________ having a party.
3. I want to go to ________ house.
4. But ________ was no address in the note.
5. ________ friends will not know where to go!

B. Circle the word in ( ) that correctly completes the sentence.

6. **(They're, There)** getting ready for the party.
7. No one comes to **(there, their)** party, though.
8. Then **(their, they're)** phone rings.
9. **(They're, Their)** going to make new notes.
10. **(Their, There)** will be a new party.

TRY THIS! Write two sentences about a party or a fun place you have been. Use *there*, *their*, or *they're* in your sentences.

Name ______________________________

Using *there, their,* and *they're*

A. Write each word from the box next to its meaning. Then add the words to the puzzle.

their	they're	there

1. that place ______________
2. belonging to them ______________
3. contraction for *they are* ______________

1. 2. 3.

B. Write *there, their,* or *they're* to complete each sentence.

4. ______________ planning a picnic.
5. Many people will be ______________.
6. That's why ______________ picnics are fun.
7. They set the food over ______________.
8. ______________ ready to eat!

TRY THIS! Write sentences using *there, their,* and *they're.* Leave out these words in each sentence. Ask a friend to fill in the blanks.

Name ______________________________

Using *to, too,* and *two*

A. Underline the word in ( ) that correctly completes the sentence.

1. **(To, Two)** days ago I went on a day trip.

2. I went **(too, to)** my uncle's cabin.

3. My grandpa was there, **(too, two)**.

4. We went **(to, too)** the lake.

5. I caught **(two, to)** fish.

B. Write *to, too,* or *two* to complete each sentence.

6. My mom caught some fish, ________.

7. ________ friends helped us carry the fish.

8. Then we headed ________ my house.

9. It took ________ hours to drive home.

10. I would go ________ the cabin again.

TRY THIS! Write rules to show how you will use *to, too,* and *two*. Then write a sentence using each word correctly.

Name ______________________________

Extra Practice

A. Circle the word in ( ) that correctly completes the sentence.

1. They got a surprise from **(there, their, they're)** mother.

2. **(There, Their, They're)** going on a trip to Texas.

3. It will be hot **(there, their, they're)**.

4. **(There, Their, They're)** plane leaves tomorrow.

B. Write *there, their,* or *they're* to complete each sentence.

5. ______________ plane flew to Dallas.

6. ______________ sitting in the front of the plane.

7. They have more space ______________.

C. Write *to, too,* or *two* to complete each sentence.

8. They went ______ a football game.

9. The ______ teams were from Texas.

10. The fans were from Texas, ______.

Name ______________________________

Using a Computer to Get Information

Write the key word or words you would use with a search engine to find the answer to each question.

1. What is the capital of England? ______________________________

2. What are three types of butterflies? ______________________________

3. Where do kangaroos live? ______________________________

4. Who is Alma Flor Ada? ______________________________

5. What does a biologist do? ______________________________

6. Where is the Golden Gate Bridge? ______________________________

7. What do bats eat? ______________________________

8. When did the Civil War begin? ______________________________

TRY THIS! Write three questions about a topic that interests you. Use a search engine to find out more information.

Developing Ideas and Topics

Brainstorm ideas for writing. Fill in the boxes. Choose one idea and tell about it.

Last summer I ______________________

____

______________________________________.

My favorite trip was to ______________

____

______________________________________.

I remember when I __________________

____

______________________________________.

Family Note: After your child reads the personal story, discuss what else the child in the story might have done (for example, take the wallet to the teacher). Then have your child complete the activity.

Fold

UNIT 1 **Grammar:** Sentences
Writing: Personal Story

Name ______________________________

by Taylor Mendez

Yesterday I was late for school. I had a reason. I found a wallet on the sidewalk. At first, I didn't know what to do. I didn't want to be late, but I didn't want to leave the wallet there.

Then I made up my mind. I picked up the wallet. I took it to the principal's office.

The principal was happy. He told me one of the students had lost the wallet. All of her money was in it. She would be very glad to get it back.

Fold

Then the principal walked me to my class. He told my teacher I had a good reason to be late. I am supposed to bring a note to my teacher if I am late. Bringing the principal was better than bringing a note!

Adding Details

List details you could use to tell a pen pal about your town or city.

Things to See
Things to Do

Family Note: After your child reads the letters, talk about things to see and do in your hometown. Then have your child complete the activity.

Fold

Name ______________________

Pen Pals

by Tara Chongyu

10 East Avenue, Apt. 2
New York, NY 10000
October 3, 2001

Dear Nico,

It's great to have a pen pal. I'll tell you all about me. I live in an apartment in New York City. I have two big brothers and one pet. I like living in a big city.

I can't wait to hear all about you. Please write soon!

Your pen pal,
Tara

17 Alamo Drive
San Antonio, TX 78000
October 17, 2001

Dear Tara,

Getting your letter was fun. I like living in a big city, too. San Antonio has a river that runs right through it. You can go there to eat lunch or shop. The Alamo is nearby. It is a famous old fort.

I have two little sisters, but I don't have a pet. Mom says it's noisy enough around here.

Please tell me more about you. What do you do in New York? What kind of pet do you have?

Your friend,
Nico

Fold

10 East Avenue, Apt. 2
New York, NY 10000
November 1, 2001

Dear Nico,

San Antonio sounds neat. New York is fun, too. We have a big park called Central Park. I play there or ride my skateboard. We have rivers, too.

Look at the picture on this paper. It shows the Statue of Liberty. The giant statue is in the harbor.

My pet is a big cat named Lucy. She likes to sit in the window and watch people.

I think you would like New York. Maybe someday you can come to see me.

Your friend,
Tara

Quotations

Find the words that Tommy said to Woody in the story. Write them below. Use quotation marks.

____

____

If Woody could speak, what would he say? Write his words. Use quotation marks.

____

____

Family Note: Ask your child what made up the beginning, the middle, and the ending of the story. Then have your child complete the activity.

Fold

UNIT 3 **Grammar:** Verbs **Writing:** Story

Name ______________________________

Woody's Big Day

by Jack Ryan

Woody the hamster was asleep. He was having his favorite dream. The dream was always the same. Woody dreamed he was out and running around in his hamster ball.

"Wake up, Woody. I have a nice surprise for you," said Tommy.

It was a big surprise! Tommy had bought a new hamster ball for Woody. Tommy put the ball on the floor. Woody climbed inside. He could see under the bed. He could see into the other room. It was a big new world.

Fold

Suddenly, Woody began to run in his ball. The ball moved fast! Woody kept running. Soon he was under the bed, but it was too dusty there. He moved over to the closet, but it was messy. He liked it under the desk best.

Woody ran around so much he got tired. He was glad when Tommy put him back in his cage. Now he could rest and dream again of running around in his very own ball.

Colorful Words

What small animal have you watched? Brainstorm colorful words that you could use to describe the animal to a friend. Can your friend guess what animal it is?

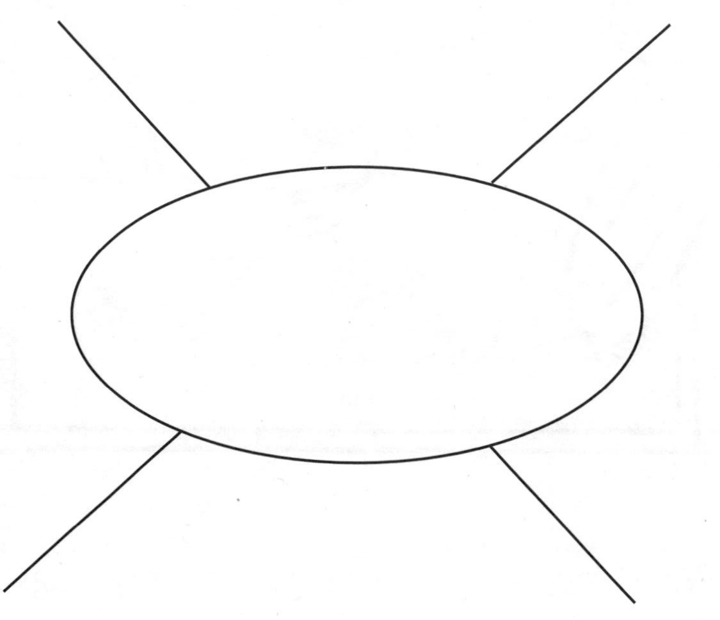

Family Note: After your child reads the description, talk about the words used to describe the frog. Then have your child color the pictures and complete the activity.

Fold

Name ______________________

My Backyard Frog

by Wayne Lewis

I have a big green frog in my backyard. He likes to sit in the sun on his favorite gray rock. He jumps in the water to cool off when his skin gets too hot.

My backyard frog is a great jumper. His long back legs give him a flying leap. His webbed feet make him a good swimmer, too.

Fold

When my backyard frog gets hungry, bugs have to hide! His long, sticky tongue darts out to catch them. Worms and spiders are favorite snacks, too. Here comes a fuzzy little spider now. Watch out!

Using Exact Words

Finish the how-to paragraph below by using exact words.

How to Make a Small Garden

To make a small garden, you will need soil, a pot, water, a spoon, and

_______________ seeds.

First, put the soil in the pot. Next, dig holes and put in the seeds. Last,

_______________ the seeds with soil and water them. Watch your

garden _______________!

Family Note: After your child reads the how-to booklet, you may want to make the beads together. Help your child review the materials and steps.

Fold

Name _______________

How to Make BEADS

by Mary Johnson

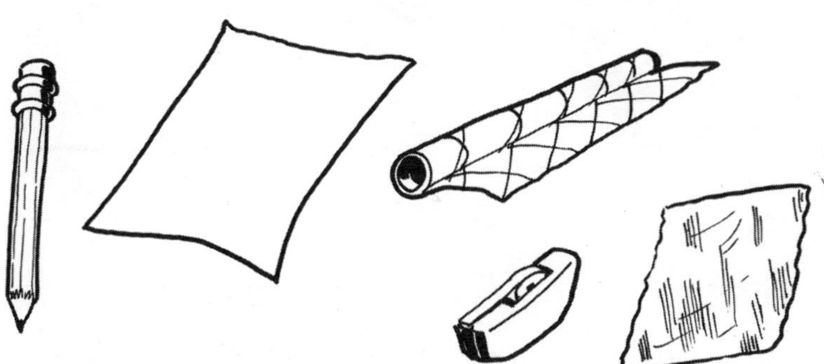

It is easy and fun to make paper beads. You will need some colored paper or gift wrap, aluminum foil, a pencil, tape, and yarn.

1.

2.

First, cut triangles and rectangles from the paper and aluminum foil. The aluminum foil makes beads that look like silver. Next, wrap the paper shape around the pencil to make the bead. Then tape the end down.

Fold

3.

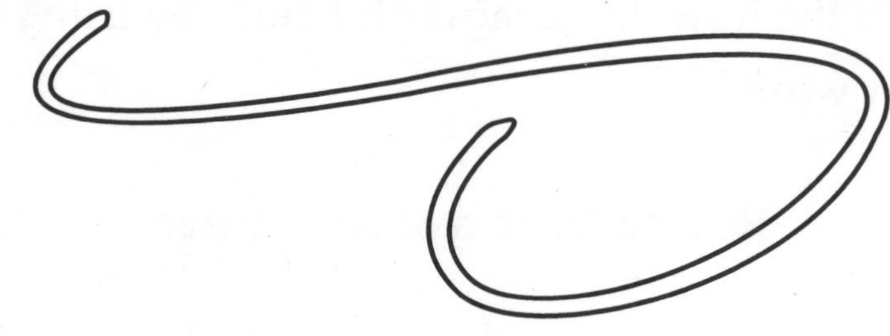

Make lots and lots of beads.

Last, string your beads on a piece of yarn for a special necklace!

Giving Examples

Write a sentence about your favorite tree. Give examples that tell what this kind of tree does for you.

Family Note: After your child reads the short report on trees, go for a nature walk. Count and identify the different kinds of trees you see. Then have your child complete the activity.

Fold

Name ____________________

Trees All Around

by Pat Lemski

There are many kinds of trees. Different kinds of trees have different kinds of leaves. Some trees, such as maples and oaks, have flat leaves. Other trees, such as pines, have leaves that look like needles.

Trees can live for a long time. Most trees live for 100 to 250 years. One kind of pine can live for more than 4,000 years!

Most people cannot tell a tree's age just by looking at it. The best way to tell a tree's age is by looking at the stump after the tree has been cut down. Then you can see its growth rings. Each ring shows one year of the tree's life.

Fold

The world is a nicer place because of trees. Trees give shade in the summer. They also make good homes for many animals and birds. People get wood from trees, too.

Skills Index

GRAMMAR

USAGE AND MECHANICS

ASSESSMENT